100

PAPER PIECED
QUILT BLOCKS

Fun foundation pieced
blocks for happy sewing

Edited by Sarah Callard

DAVID & CHARLES

www.davidandcharles.com

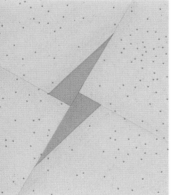

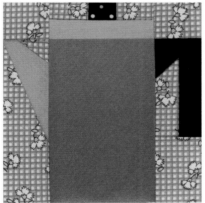

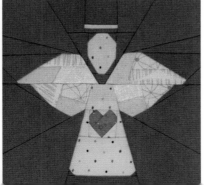

CONTENTS

INTRODUCTION

The technique of foundation paper piecing is where fabric is sewn directly onto a paper foundation. The paper is there to provide stability. It stops fabric from warping (even when sewn on the bias) and it allows pieces to be sewn that are considerably smaller and more awkwardly shaped than would normally be considered in quilting. The stitching is done on a sewing machine using tiny stitches that perforate and weaken the paper. When the sewing is complete, the paper is peeled away, leaving a beautiful piece of patchwork.

The range of different designs that can be achieved using foundation paper piecing is explored in this delightful collection. There are a total of 100 finished blocks from eleven talented designers embracing popular everyday themes, including food and drink, hobbies and leisure, and celebrations. The finished 6" (15.5cm) blocks can be incorporated into quilt designs, of course, but we wanted to give you a few other project ideas too, so there are ten to get you started.

If this is your first time using the foundation paper piecing technique, the Paper Piecing Technique chapter will have all the information you need. But even if you have experience of this method of patchwork, it's worth taking the time to review this section as there are lots of tips for perfecting your skills. Enjoy!

HOW TO USE THIS BOOK

The main aim of this book is to present a collection of 100 paper pieced blocks for you to pick and choose from, to incorporate into your quilting and sewing projects. The instructions for making each block are presented as shown here:

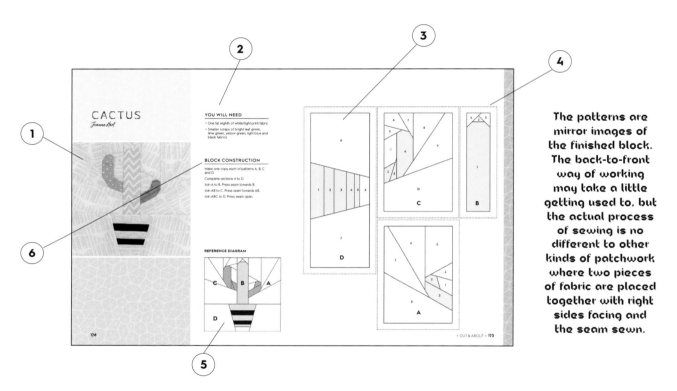

1 Photograph of the finished block: each block measures 6½" x 6½" (16.5cm x 16.5cm) which includes seam allowances, but this photo shows how the block will look once the block is used in a quilt or sewing project (i.e. without seam allowances).

2 You Will Need: this lists all the fabric requirements to make the block, starting always with the background fabric. Specific measurements are provided wherever a piece of fabric is required that measures 6" (15.5cm) or more in either dimension. If no specific measurement is given, you can safely assume that smaller scraps than this are required.

3 Block patterns: reproduced actual size, these show the design in reverse. Note that when paper piecing, the fabric is sewn to the **back** of the paper pattern so the stitched sections are mirror images of the patterns.

The Cactus Block shown here has four patterns, A, B, C and D. Each number on each pattern piece refers to a fabric piece, and the fabrics are sewn together in numerical order, starting with fabric piece 1.

4 Each pattern has a ¼" (6mm) seam allowance around the edge as indicated by the dashed line.

5 Reference diagram: this shows both the placement of the fabrics and how the pieced sections fit together to make the finished block (completed fabric-side view). Red lines indicate where the sections are joined. The order of joining of the pieced sections is outlined in the Block Construction text.

6 Block Construction: this gives step-by-step instruction for sewing the pieced sections together to complete the finished block, including how to press the sewn seams for neatest results.

PAPER PIECING TECHNIQUES

In this chapter, the basics of making foundation paper pieced quilt blocks are explained, with extra tips on perfecting your technique. If you are new to this method of working, do read through this section several times before making a start on your first block.

COPYING THE PATTERNS

The first thing to do is to make a copy of the patterns for your chosen block. While it is possible to use a thin 80gsm-weight printer paper, buying paper specially made for foundation paper piecing does have some advantages: it is easier to see through and quicker to tear away at the end of sewing, while limiting the risk of pulling out stitches – although it will be more expensive, of course!

The patterns for the blocks can be downloaded from www.davidandcharles.com. It is important to check your printer settings every time you print, otherwise your finished block may end up with the wrong dimensions. Where possible, print from a computer as phones and tablets often offer little control over printer settings. The exact wording used in print preferences settings can vary greatly depending on your printer and the software you are using. You need to print using 'print 100%' or 'Actual Size'. Do not use 'Shrink to Size' or 'Fit to Page'. Where possible, open the PDF in Adobe Acrobat Reader, as this gives clear, unambiguous printing options.

Check the test 1" square has been printed correctly before cutting out your patterns ready to start sewing. This will enable you to quickly check that your pattern has not been accidentally reduced in size.

Once you are confident that the patterns have printed out to size, cut each pattern out along the dashed line.

Make a second copy of your patterns onto standard copy paper and colour in the sections to help you remember which fabric goes where, crossing out each piece on this guide as you sew it.

STITCH LENGTH

When you are ready to start paper piecing, you will need to reduce the length of your stitches. Stitch sizes can vary depending on the sewing machine, but for most machines aim for a stitch length between 1.5 and 2. The stitches should be close together, but not so close that they shred the paper. The small stitch length creates a line of small perforations along the paper, meaning that there is minimal strain placed on the stitches when the paper is torn away.

CUTTING FABRIC PIECES

Fabric cut for paper piecing should be approximately ½" (1.3cm) larger than the printed shape on the paper pattern but you don't need to cut the pieces precisely. It can be useful to cut rectangles of fabric, then reuse the scraps later in your project (or for another block) to minimise wastage. Some people like to cut all their fabric before they piece; others prefer to cut as they sew, the choice is yours. It may, however, be sensible to cut out the largest pieces first and to use the remainder of the fabric (and cut-offs) for smaller pieces to ensure that you do not run out of your preferred fabric choice.

Not all the lettered sections that make up a block have to be pieced. Sometimes just a single piece of fabric needs to be cut in preparation to be sewn to the other sections in the construction of the block, as can be seen in pattern pieces C, D, I, J and K on the New Home Block (see Celebrations).

COMPLETING THE PAPER PIECED SECTIONS

Red thread is used in the photos shown in this and the following sections, so stitches can be seen clearly.

1 Placing fabric piece 1

Place the paper pattern printed side down on the table or light box. Place the fabric for piece 1 right side up on top of the foundation paper pattern. If you are not using a light box, hold the paper and fabric up to the light with the paper pattern towards you, so that you can clearly see the printed lines and the outlines of the fabric pieces. Ensure that the fabric overlaps the edges of piece 1 by at least ¼" (6mm) in all directions (Photo 1). If piece 1 is next to the printed seam allowance, the fabric should also cover the seam allowance. When you are satisfied with the positioning of your fabric, pin to hold it in place.

Place the pin far enough away from the line between pieces, so it can stay in place while you are sewing the seam.

2 Align the next fabric piece

Place the fabric for piece 2 right side down on top of fabric piece 1 (Photo 2). Carefully lift the whole pile up to the light (or use the light box) to check that the majority of the fabric is on top of piece 1, but that the edge overlaps the printed line between piece 1 and 2 by more than ¼" (6mm). Check the position in one of the following ways:

* Gently fold the fabric of piece 2 back with your fingers. This can be a bit tricky to do if you are not used to it.

* Place a pin along the line that you are going to sew and then fold the fabric of piece 2 back.

* Machine tack the seam using a longer stitch length (size 4 or larger) first. This is particularly useful for fussy cut fabrics. If you are not happy, then you can easily unpick the stitches and resew without worrying that you have weakened your paper foundation.

If machine tacking, don't forget to reset your machine to resew the seam with small stitches!

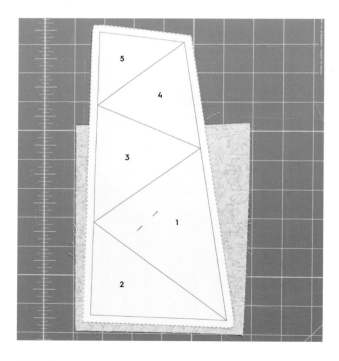

Photo 1

Photo 2

3 Sew the fabric pieces together

Carefully manoeuvre your pile of fabric and paper into your sewing machine, printed paper side up, taking care that none of the fabrics move. You are going to sew down the line between piece 1 and piece 2 (Photo 3). It is important that you anchor your stitches so that they do not come undone when you remove the paper. There are a couple of ways to do this, although a combination of the two is often the answer:

* Start and end your seams with a few backwards stitches. The disadvantage of this technique is that it makes the first few stitches harder to unpick if you make a mistake.

* Start and finish your seam up to a ¼" (6mm) past the end of the line. When you do this, you will need to rip the paper slightly when you fold it to trim the fabrics afterwards. This may not be suitable for areas of very small piecing.

If the line being sewn starts or finishes by the ¼" (6mm) seam allowance, extend the line of stitches into it, then trim thread to the paper.

4 Flip and check

Gently fold the fabric for piece 2 over (Photo 4). Hold it up to the light and ensure that it generously covers printed shape 2, allowing at least ¼" (6mm) seam allowances. If it doesn't, carefully unpick. If it does, then unfold fabric piece 2 to let it lie on top of piece 1 again. Do not press yet.

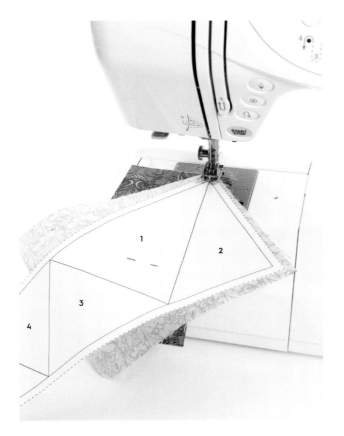

Photo 3

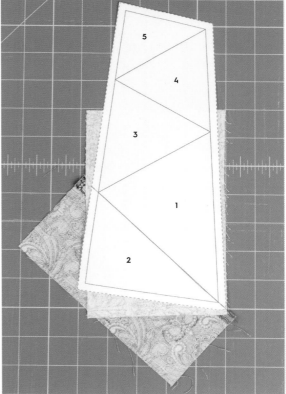

Photo 4

5 Trimming the sewn seams

Ensuring that the two pieces of fabric that have just been sewn are lying with right sides facing each other, fold the paper back along the stitched lines so that the seam allowances are exposed. Place the ruler along the seam and trim the edges, allowing a ¼" (6mm) seam allowance. Photo 5 shows an Add-A-Quarter ruler being used, but a normal quilting ruler works fine. Once the seams have been trimmed, unfold your paper so that it lies flat again.

6 Pressing the pieced seams

When pressing the seams, use a dry iron: steam can distort the fabric and paper, and can lead to printed paper losing its ink, smudging black marks all over your sewing. It is a good idea to set the seam when pressing: first, press the seam flat on the back of the fabric in the position that you have just sewn it (Photo 6); then, open the seam and press again from the front (Photo 7). You can gently finger press the seam open before you press, to ensure that the crease lands in the correct spot.

7 Repeat to complete the piecing

Repeat the basic process from Step 2, until you have sewn all the fabric pieces to the paper pattern. Repeat the piecing process on all of the paper patterns to complete the sections that make up the block design. Once all the fabrics have been sewn to the paper patterns, trim the fabrics to the seam allowance (i.e. the outer dashed line on each pattern). If it is essential that the finished block is exactly the right size, do not trim the outer edge of the block until all the sections have been sewn together (see Joining the Paper Pieced Sections Together).

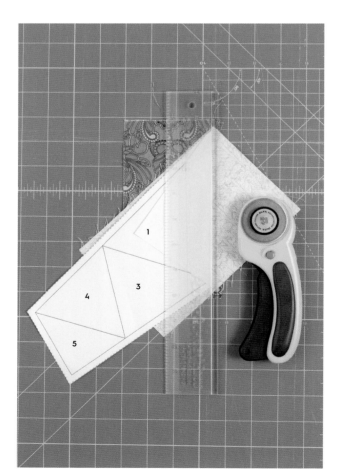

Photo 5

Photo 6

Photo 7

PERFECTING THE PAPER PIECING TECHNIQUE

We have now covered the basics of paper piecing, but there are definitely some aspects of the technique that take more practice than others as we will explore here.

Sewing awkward angles

1 Cut a piece of fabric that is at least ½" (1.3cm) larger in all directions than the area you want to cover. Lay your pattern printed side up and the fabric rectangle right side down on the printed side of the pattern, ensuring it generously covers the section that you want to sew including seam allowances. Fold the fabric along the seam that you are going to sew and press (Photo 8). Take note of the position of the fabric in relation to the pattern (the dashed line indicates the pattern edges). It is important to know how much fabric overhang there is at either end, as this will help you position the fabric correctly against the non-printed side of the pattern. You may choose to mark the ends of the section on the fabric with a fabric marker.

2 Now take the fabric and position it in situ against the non-printed side of the pattern (Photo 9). Remember that it will be placed right sides together with the fabric of the area adjacent to the area you are about to cover. Hold it up to the light and check that the fold of the fabric follows the line that you are about to sew. When happy with the positioning, flick the fold of the fabric open (Photo 10) and then position the whole bundle in your sewing machine ready to sew, pattern side facing up (Photo 11). In cases where you are piecing an area next to the edge of the paper and the fabric that you are about to sew is visible around the edges of the pattern, it is possible to make a final check on fabric alignment. Look for the crease that was created when you pressed the fabric and check whether it is still in alignment with the printed line. If you look at Photo 11 you will see that the fabric needs to be moved a couple of millimetres to the right (see arrow).

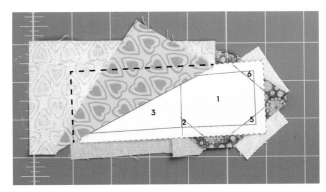

Photo 8

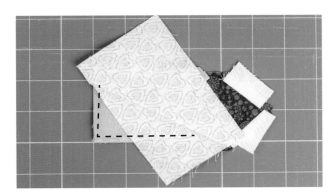

Photo 10

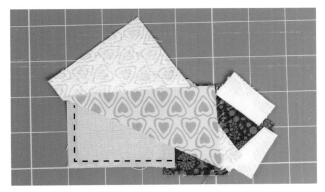

Photo 9

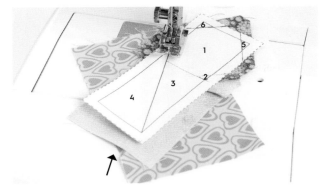

Photo 11

3 Sew along the line with a large machine tacking stitch (Photo 12). Check whether the fabric piece has been orientated correctly. If not, unpick the stitches and try again. If it has been sewn correctly, resew the line using your normal small paper piecing stitches.

Sewing with directional prints

When sewing with directional prints, such as with the formula print on the Measuring Jug and the strawberry print on the Jam Jar (see Kitchen), stop and think about the direction you want the print to go before you start sewing, and if accurate alignment is important, follow these steps:

1 Lay the paper pattern out in its correct orientation. Draw an arrow pointing straight up towards the upper edge of the paper. This arrow will act as a constant reminder as to where the top of the block lies. Now draw a horizontal line intersecting the arrowed line that can be used as a reference for accurate alignment.

2 Cut fabric generously, bearing its orientation in mind. Lay the pattern print side up and lay the fabric right side down over the area that you wish to sew. Use the drawn reference line to help orientate the fabric accurately. Fold the seam allowance along the line that you will sew. Press to create a nice clean edge.

3 Move the fabric to the non-printed side of the template. Hold paper and fabric up to a light source and align the fold with the printed line. Sew using machine tacking stitches.

4 Check that the alignment is accurate and resew the seam using small stitches.

Working with small fabric pieces

When the first two pieces of fabric to be sewn to a pattern are small, the stitches can sometimes rip away from the paper, leading to frustration and resewing. Here are some simple steps to avoid this:

1 Cut your fabric generously. Be sure to use a pin to anchor fabric piece 1 to the paper pattern and if possible try to ensure that this pin can remain in situ until the seam between piece 2 and 3 has been sewn (Photo 13). As there will only be a small number of stitches holding the fabric to the paper, this pin serves to take some of the strain off the seam between piece 1 and piece 2 and means that there is less chance that the stitches will rip away from the paper.

2 Start the seam one or two stitches before the line begins and extend it one or two stitches past the end. These few extra stitches can make all the difference in anchoring the fabric to the paper.

3 Take care when folding the fabric, as there are only a few anchor stitches and it's easy to misalign the fold.

> To reduce bulk, especially when there are a lot of small pieces in one area, it is possible to trim the seam allowances slightly narrower making them between ⅛" (3mm) and ¼" (6mm).

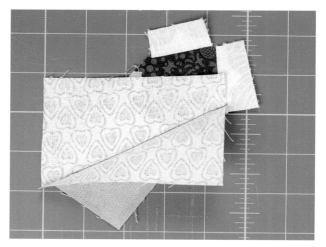

Photo 12

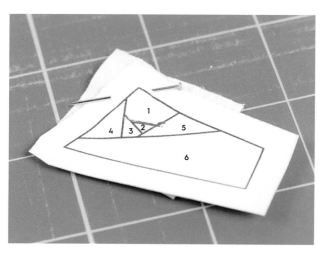

Photo 13

JOINING THE PAPER PIECED SECTIONS TOGETHER

With just a handful of exceptions, the paper-pieced blocks in this book consist of more than one section (lettered A, B, C, etc). These must be sewn together in the order specified in Block Construction.

❯ First, analyse the design. You will notice that there are some sections that can easily be sewn together without any need for precision, while others require significantly more attention to detail. Look for the critical joining points – these are the points that need to match precisely when they are sewn together. Examples of these joining points for the Owl Block are shown by red circles in Fig 1. Some blocks will have no critical joining points and the Cactus Block is a good example of that.

❷ Once you have identified a critical joining point, push a pin through the paper and straight through to the fabric (Photo 14). Make sure that the pin comes out directly adjacent to the crease of the seam (Photo 15).

If you use a walking foot when joining sections together, the papers are less likely to slip in relation to each other and alignment is just that bit more accurate when sewn this way.

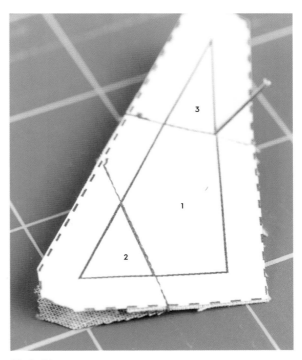

Photo 14

Fig 1

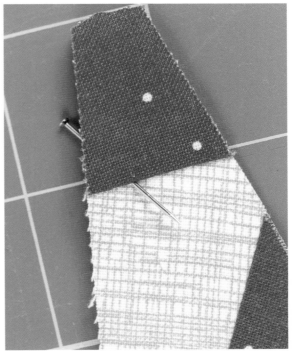

Photo 15

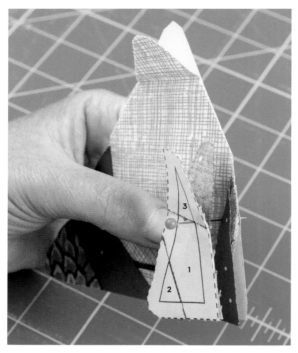

Photo 16

3 Now take the other paper pieced section and continue to push the pin through the crease of the fabric and the paper (Photo 16). Now the pin should be standing perpendicular to the papers, which are sandwiched together with fabric in the centre (Photo 17). We can call this pin the anchor pin. If you now take the anchor pin and push it through the paper horizontally, you will notice that the papers shift on top of each other and are no longer beautifully lined up (Photo 18). Even the slightest movement of the papers at this stage can make a huge difference to the accuracy of your join. As a result, you need to leave the anchor pin standing perpendicular to the fabric for the moment.

4 Use clips or pins to anchor the papers together on either side of the anchor pin before removing it. If there are several critical anchor points along one seam, place anchor pins on every one of these points. Anchor pins can also be helpful at the start and finish of seams, especially when sewing a section with an acute angle.

Clips hold sections together without shifting, which sometimes happens when pinning.

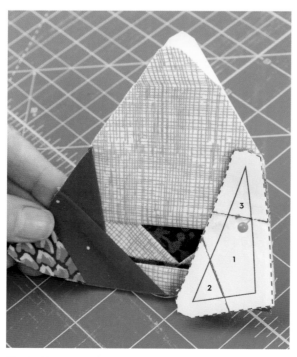

Photo 17

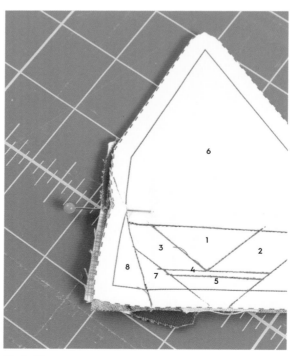

Photo 18

5 When sewing seams with critical joining points, use a longer machine tacking stitch to test the alignment before sewing with your shorter foundation paper piecing stitch. That way, if the sections do not align to your liking, the stitches will be much quicker and easier to remove. Try to sew as accurately as possible and to keep all stitches exactly on the printed line. Start sewing from the end closest to the first anchor pin. The shorter the distance that you have to sew before crossing an anchor point, the smaller the chance that slippage will occur and the more accurately you will sew.

6 Press the seams between sections as advised, but note that the sections will almost always decide for themselves which way that they want to lie. That said, at times (especially when the critical join point falls on a steeply angled seam where there is a lot of bulk), you may find that a seam has been joined accurately, but doesn't look right. If the seam allowance has been pressed closed, opening the seam to share the bulk between the two sides of the seam may make the difference you are looking for.

> To make it easier to remove the papers from the finished block, rip about 1" (2.5cm) of paper away from the ends of the seam allowances once two sections have been sewn together.

Nesting seams

Nesting seams helps to reduce bulk where multiple seams meet, allowing the sections of a block to join more accurately. It applies to seams that run perpendicular to a new seam to be sewn. For the seams to nest, press the seams of the two sections to be joined in opposite directions. For example, if you are joining a left and right side of a symmetrical block, you will press the seams on one side towards the top of the block and those on the other side towards the bottom of the block. When you line these two sections up to join them, their seams will 'slot' into each other. This allows the new seam to lie flatter, and the nested seams help prevent block distortion as you sew.

REMOVING THE PAPERS

Only remove the papers once you have finished sewing all of the sections of the block together and you are ready to incorporate the block into a quilt or to use it for one of the project ideas we have supplied. Remember that a paper-pieced block can be vulnerable to warping as the fabrics are generally sewn in all directions, so take your time and do it gently, ripping away the pieces in reverse number order. It can be helpful to have a pair of tweezers or a quick unpick to help ease some of the smaller paper pieces out of the seams.

FINISHING A BLOCK

When a block is finished, it can appear a bit lumpy along the seams, particularly at points where multiple seams join up. A final step can help to flatten your seams out. Once all the papers are removed and with the block wrong side facing up, check that the seams are pressed in the directions that you want them to be; if not, press them quickly into position. Now lay several layers of wadding on your ironing board. Place your block on top of the wadding with the right side facing up. Spray the block generously with starch or starch equivalent, then press the block until it is dry. The block becomes beautifully flat, with crisp seams, and using starch has the added bonus of protecting it from warping.

Resizing patterns

One of the fun things about paper-pieced patterns is that it is relatively easy to alter the dimensions of a pattern. To alter the pattern to a different block size, the basic equation for working out the change of scale required when printing out the patterns is:

what you want (required block size) ÷ what you have (current block size) x 100

However, remember that increasing or decreasing a pattern will alter the size of the whole pattern, including the ¼" (6mm) seam allowance. It is very important therefore to manually change the seam allowances back to ¼" (6mm).

SHED

Sarah Ashford

YOU WILL NEED

- Large scrap of dark green fabric, at least 6" x 9" (15.5cm x 23cm)
- Smaller scraps of mid green, light green and light brown fabrics
- Small orange button

BLOCK CONSTRUCTION

Make one copy each of patterns A, B and C.

Complete sections A to C.

Join B to C. Press seam open.

Join BC to A. Press seams towards BC.

Sew the button door handle onto the door of the finished block.

REFERENCE DIAGRAM

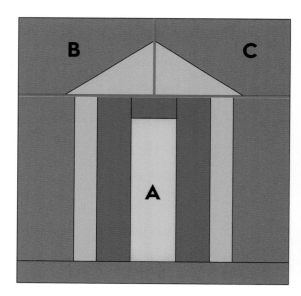

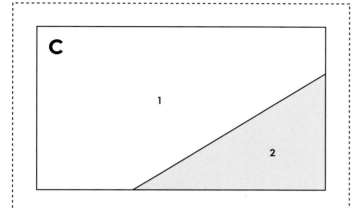

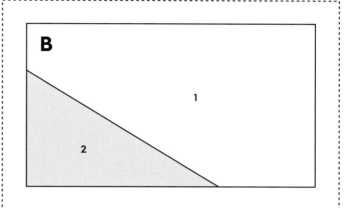

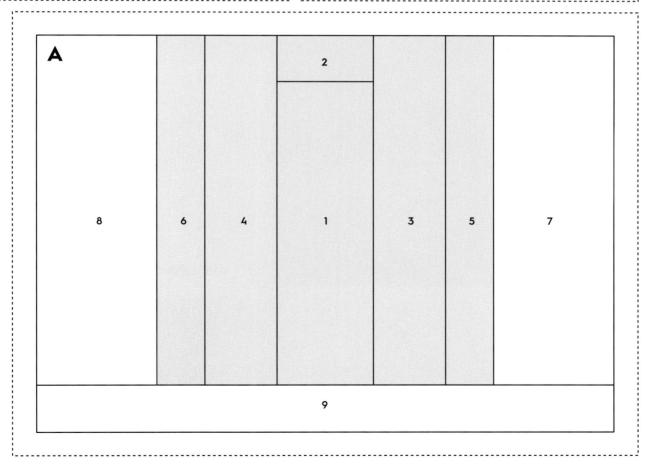

TREE
Sarah Ashford

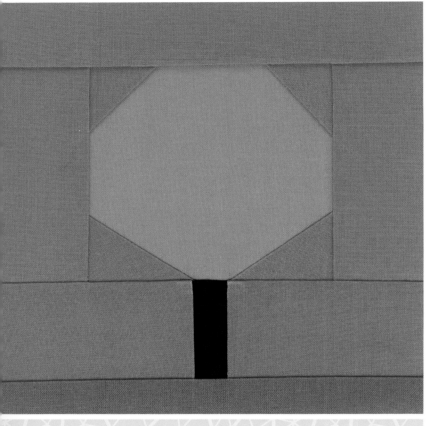

YOU WILL NEED

* Large scrap of light blue fabric, at least 10" x 9" (25.5cm x 23cm)
* Strip of mid green fabric, at least 7" x 1½" (18cm x 4cm)
* Smaller scraps of light green and brown fabrics

BLOCK CONSTRUCTION

Make one copy each of patterns A and B.

Complete sections A to B.

Join A to B. Press seam towards B.

REFERENCE DIAGRAM

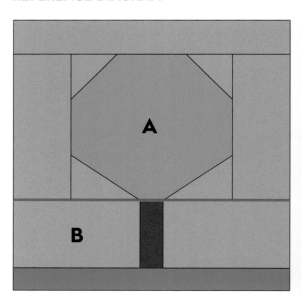

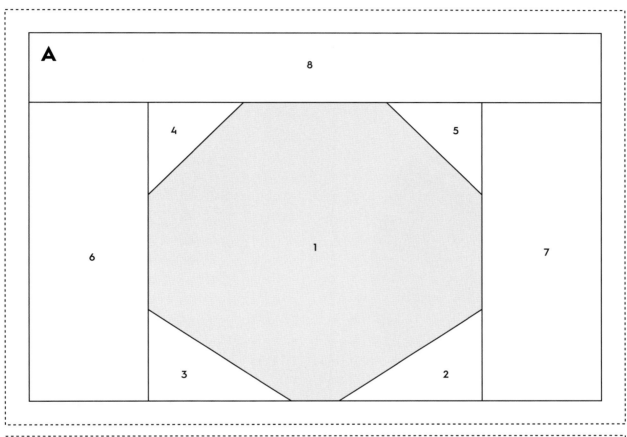

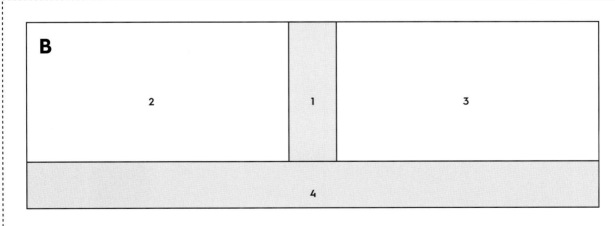

LEAF
Kitty Wilkin

YOU WILL NEED

- Large scrap of white fabric, at least 11" x 15" (28cm x 38cm)
- Smaller scraps of green fabrics, seven lighter and seven darker shades

BLOCK CONSTRUCTION

Make one copy each of patterns A and B.

Complete sections A to B, using lighter shades on section A and darker shades on section B.

Join A to B. Press seam open.

REFERENCE DIAGRAM

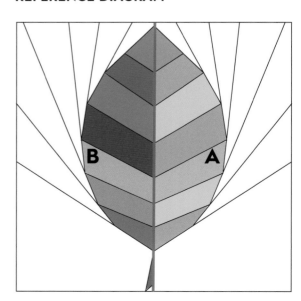

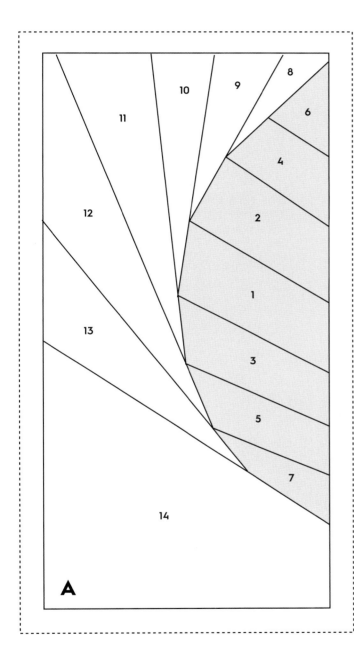

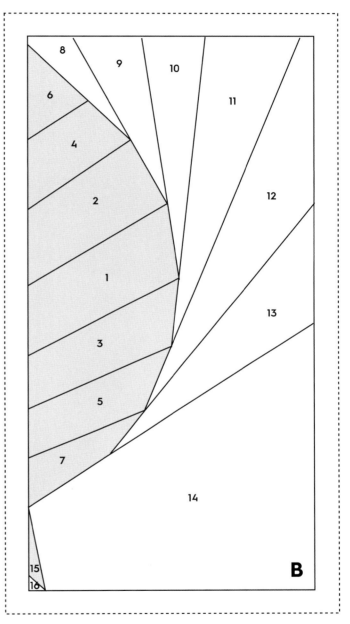

TOADSTOOL

Lindsay Chieco

YOU WILL NEED

* Large scrap of blue fabric, at least 11" x 11" (28cm x 28cm)
* Large scrap of red fabric, at least 4" x 6" (10cm x 15.5cm)
* Smaller scrap of light tan fabric

BLOCK CONSTRUCTION

Make one copy each of patterns A, B, C and D.

Complete sections A to D.

Join C to A. Press seam towards A.

Join CA to B. Press seam towards CA.

Join CAB to D. Press seam towards CAB.

REFERENCE DIAGRAM

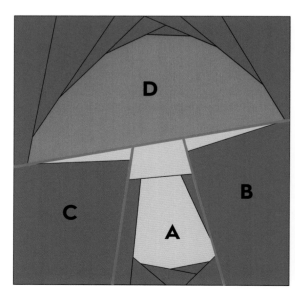

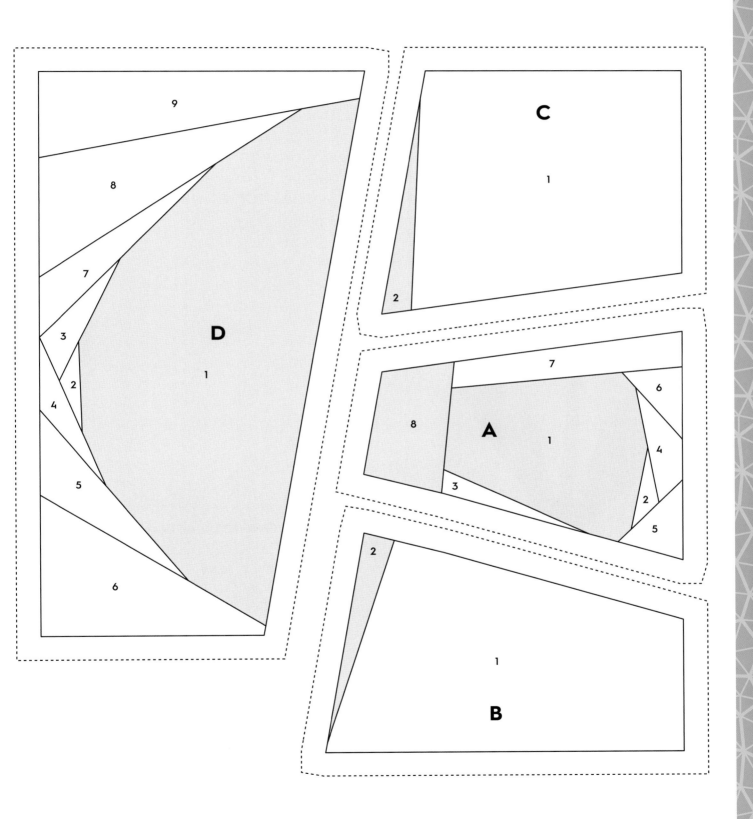

TULIP

Kitty Wilkin

YOU WILL NEED

* Large scrap of white fabric, at least 10"
  x 15" (25.5cm x 38cm)
* Smaller scraps of four pink and two
  green fabrics in slightly varied shades

BLOCK CONSTRUCTION

Make one copy each of patterns A, B
and C.

Complete sections A to C.

Join B to C. Press seam open.

Join A to BC. Press seam open.

REFERENCE DIAGRAM

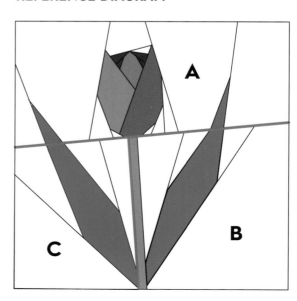

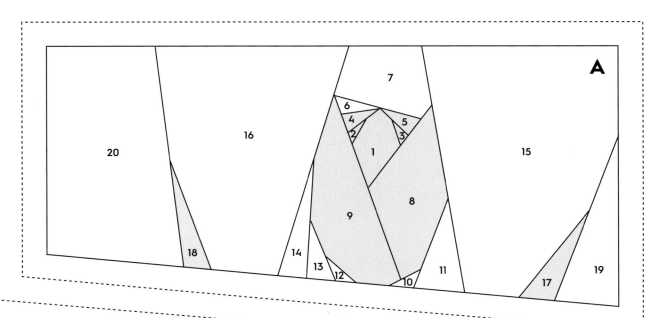

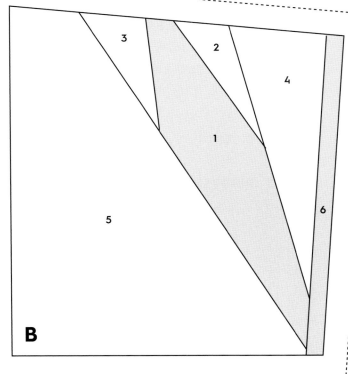

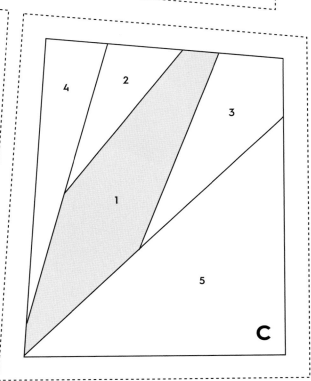

VIOLET

Kitty Wilkin

YOU WILL NEED

* Large scrap of white fabric, at least 12" x 15" (30.5cm x 38cm)
* Smaller scraps of yellow, violet and assorted green fabrics

BLOCK CONSTRUCTION

Make one copy each of patterns A, B, C, D, E, F, G and H.

Complete sections A to H.

Join A to B. Press seam open.

Join C to D. Press seam open.

Join CD to E. Press seam open.

Join AB to CDE. Press seam open.

Join F to G. Press seam open.

Join ABCDE to FG. Press seam open.

Join ABCDEFG to H. Press seam open.

REFERENCE DIAGRAM

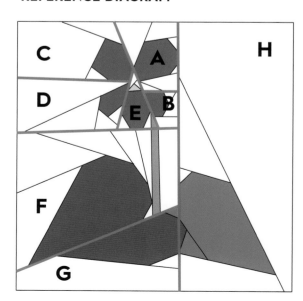

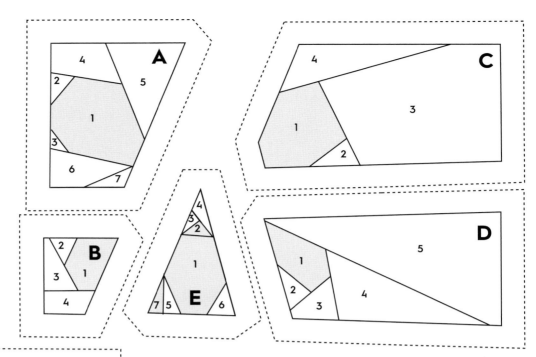

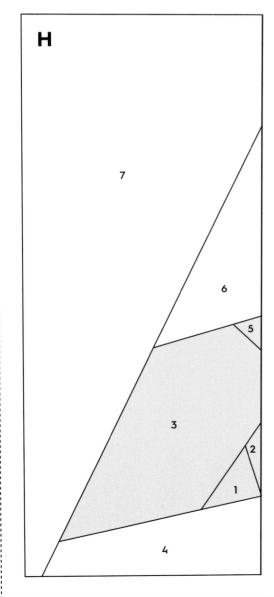

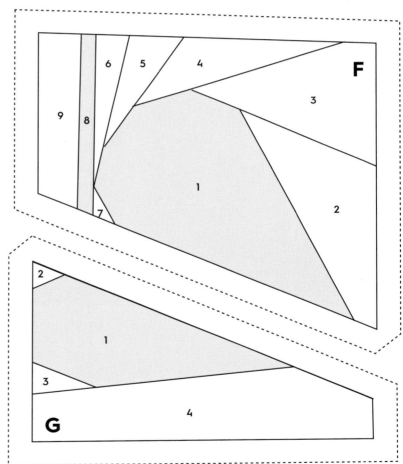

RETRO BLOOM

Sarah Ashford

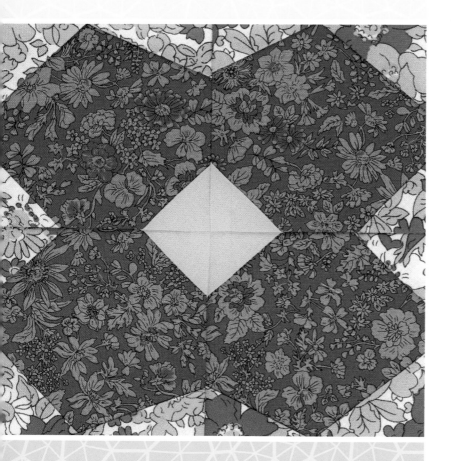

YOU WILL NEED

- Large scrap of blue print fabric, at least 8" x 8" (20.5cm x 20.5cm)
- Large scrap of multicolour floral print fabric, at least 8" x 6" (20.5cm x 15.5cm)
- Smaller scrap of yellow fabric

BLOCK CONSTRUCTION

Make one copy each of patterns A, B, C and D.

Complete sections A to D.

Join A to B. Press seam towards A.

Join C to D. Press seam towards C.

Join AB to CD. Press seam towards AB.

REFERENCE DIAGRAM

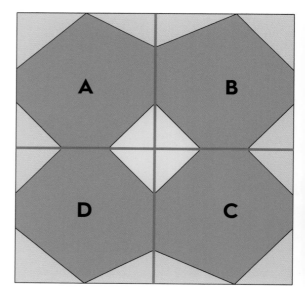

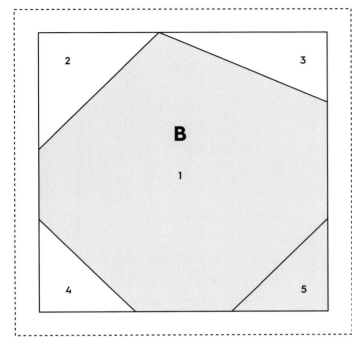

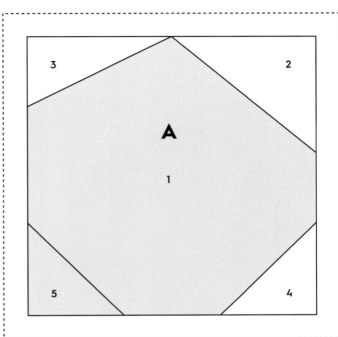

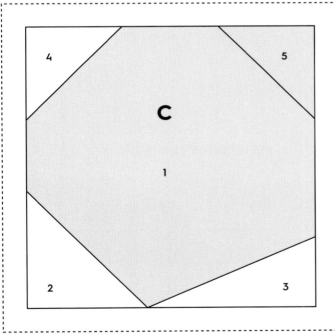

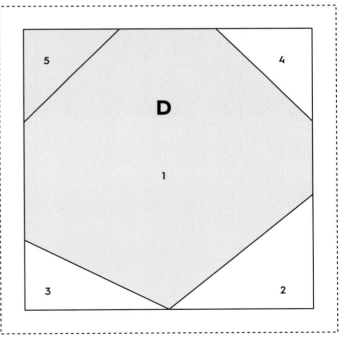

BEEHIVE

Joanne Hart

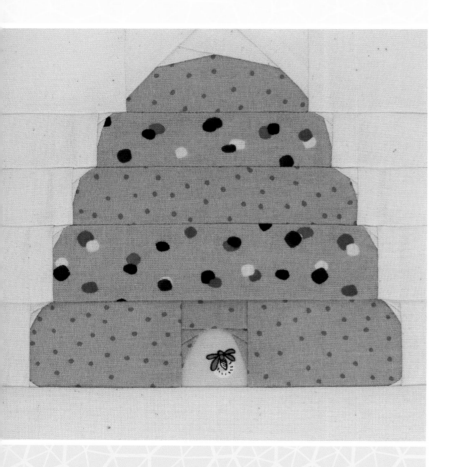

YOU WILL NEED

- One fat eighth of cream fabric
- Smaller scraps of assorted yellow fabrics and a fussy cut bee print fabric

BLOCK CONSTRUCTION

Make one copy each of patterns A, B, C, D and E.

Complete sections A to E.

Join A to B. Press seam towards B.

Join AB to C. Press seam towards AB.

Join ABC to D. Press seam towards ABC.

Join ABCD to E. Press seam towards ABCD.

REFERENCE DIAGRAM

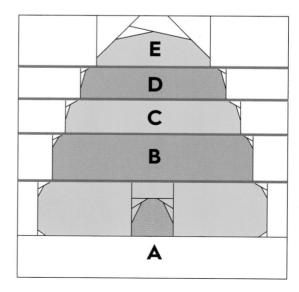

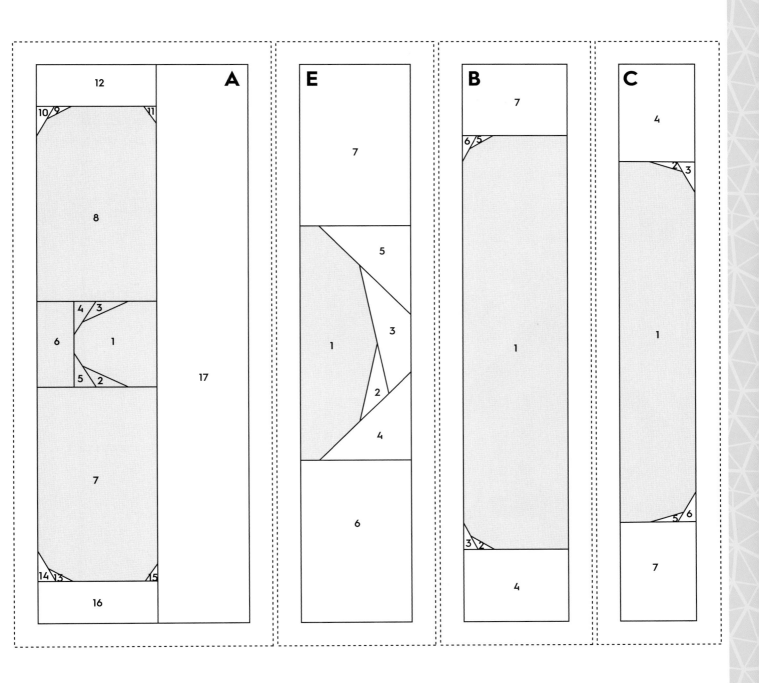

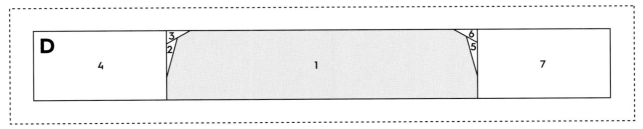

BIRDHOUSE

Kristy Lea

YOU WILL NEED

- One fat eighth of white/light print fabric
- Large scrap of aqua fabric, at least 1½" x 20" (4cm x 51cm)
- Smaller scraps of dark blue, black, yellow, pink and orange fabrics

BLOCK CONSTRUCTION

Make one copy each of patterns A, B, C, D and E.

Complete sections A to E.

Join A to B. Press seam towards B.

Join C to D. Press seam towards D.

Join CD to E. Press seam towards CD.

Join AB to CDE. Press seam towards CDE.

REFERENCE DIAGRAM

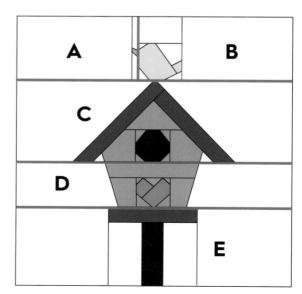

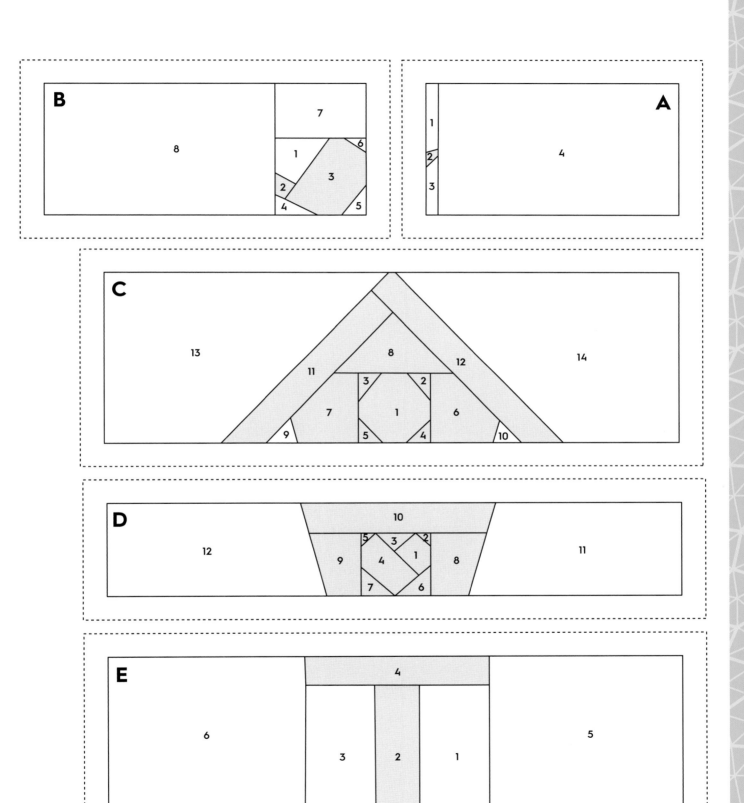

FEATHER

Joanne Hart

YOU WILL NEED

- One fat eighth of cream fabric
- Smaller scraps of bright yellow, mid yellow, orange, pink, red, blue, green and purple fabrics

BLOCK CONSTRUCTION

Make one copy each of patterns A and B.

Complete sections A and B.

Join A to B. Press seams open.

REFERENCE DIAGRAM

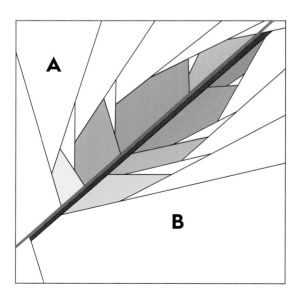

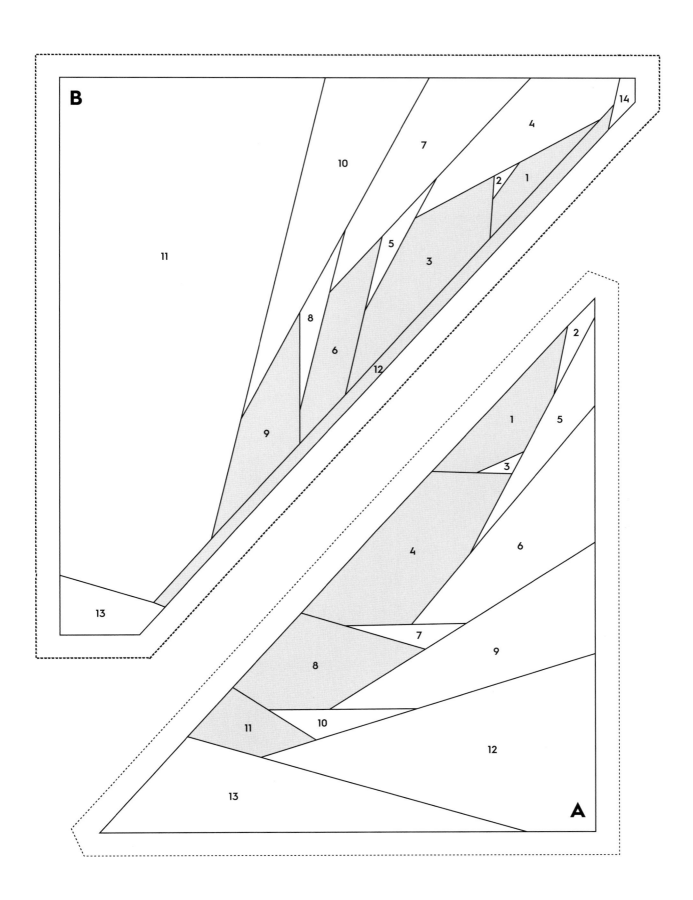

PUPPY
Jo Carter

YOU WILL NEED

* Large scrap of yellow fabric, at least 10" x 10" (25.5cm x 25.5cm)
* Large scrap of tan fabric, at least 9" x 9" (23cm x 23cm)
* Large scrap of brown fabric, at least 7" x 7" (18cm x 18cm)
* Smaller scraps of black, white and mid pink fabrics

BLOCK CONSTRUCTION

Make one copy each of patterns A, B, C, D, E and F.

Complete sections A to F.

Join A to B. Press seam open.

Join AB to C. Press seam towards C.

Join ABC to D. Press seam towards D.

Join ABCD to E. Press seam towards E.

Join ABCDE to F. Press seam towards F.

REFERENCE DIAGRAM

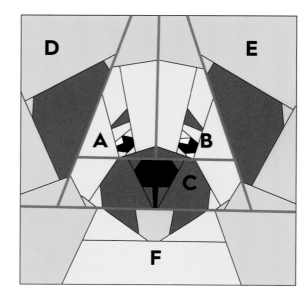

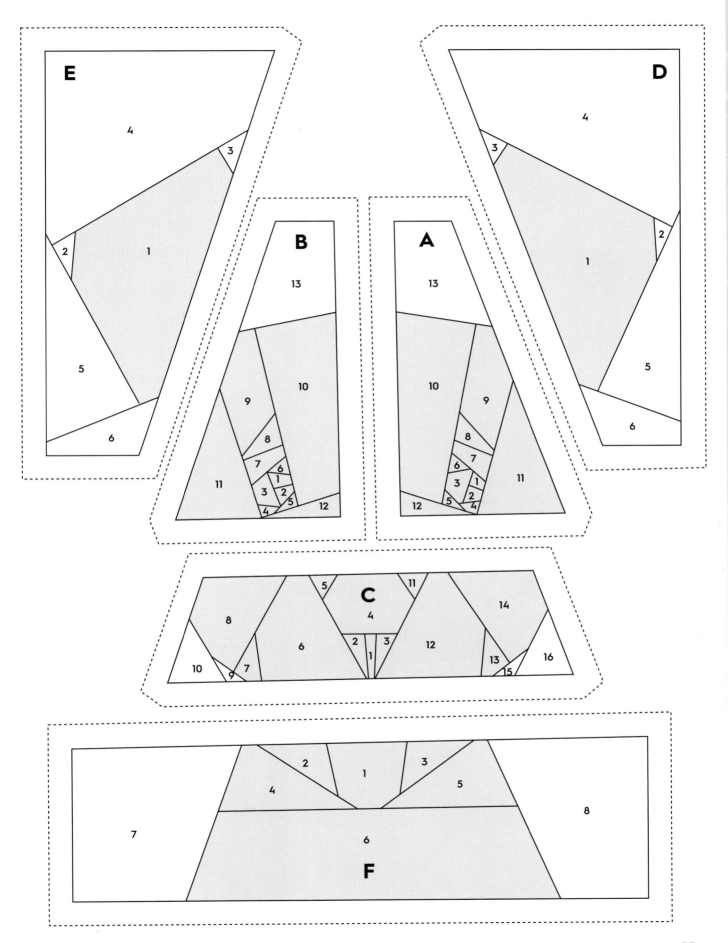

KITTEN
Jo Carter

YOU WILL NEED

- Large scrap of light teal fabric, at least 9" x 9" (23cm x 23cm)
- Large scrap of grey fabric, at least 9" x 9" (23cm x 23cm)
- Large scrap of green fabric, at least 5" x 6" (13cm x 15.5cm)
- Smaller scraps of light pink, black and white fabrics

BLOCK CONSTRUCTION

Make one copy each of patterns A, B, C, D, E, F and G.

Complete sections A to G.

Join A to B. Press seam towards A.

Join AB to C. Press seam towards AB.

Join D to E. Press seam towards E.

Join F to G. Press seam towards G.

Join DE to FG. Press seam open.

Join ABC to DEFG. Press seam towards DEFG.

REFERENCE DIAGRAM

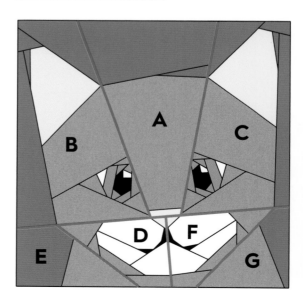

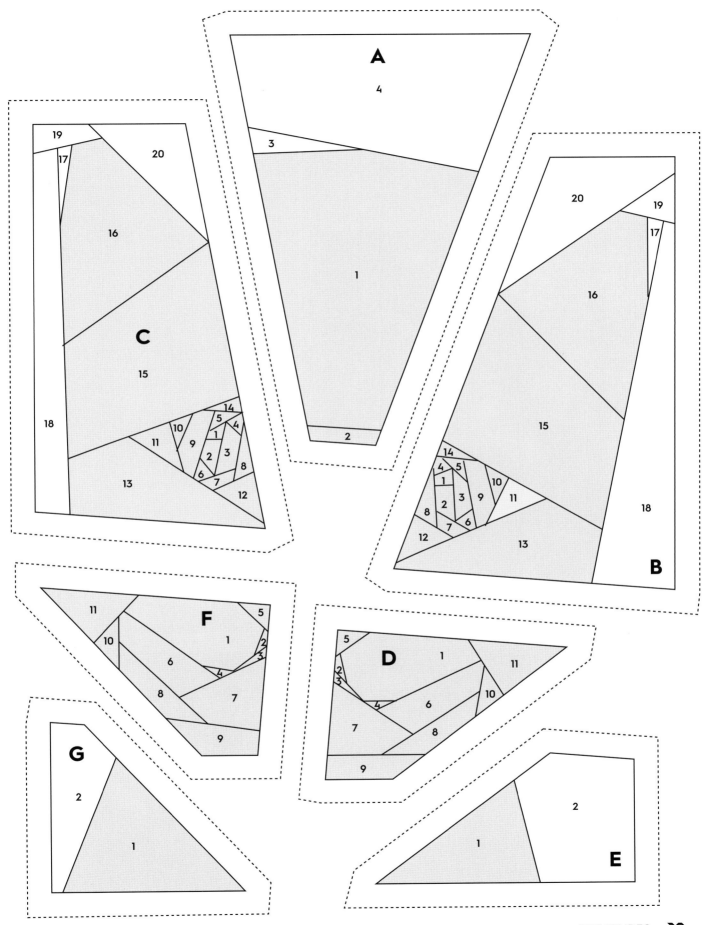

CROCODILE

Juliet van der Heijden

YOU WILL NEED

- One fat eighth of purple fabric
- Large scrap of mid green fabric, at least 10" x 10" (25.5cm x 25.5cm)
- Large scrap of bright green fabric, at least 10" x 10" (25.5cm x 25.5cm)
- Smaller scraps of lime green, yellow, black and white fabrics

BLOCK CONSTRUCTION

Make one copy each of patterns A, B, C and D.

Complete sections A to D.

Join A to B. Press seam open

Join AB to C. Press seam open.

Join ABC to D. Press seam open.

REFERENCE DIAGRAM

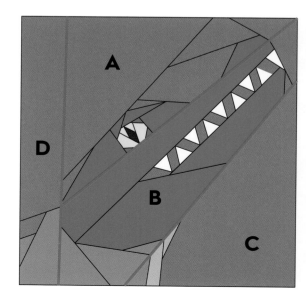

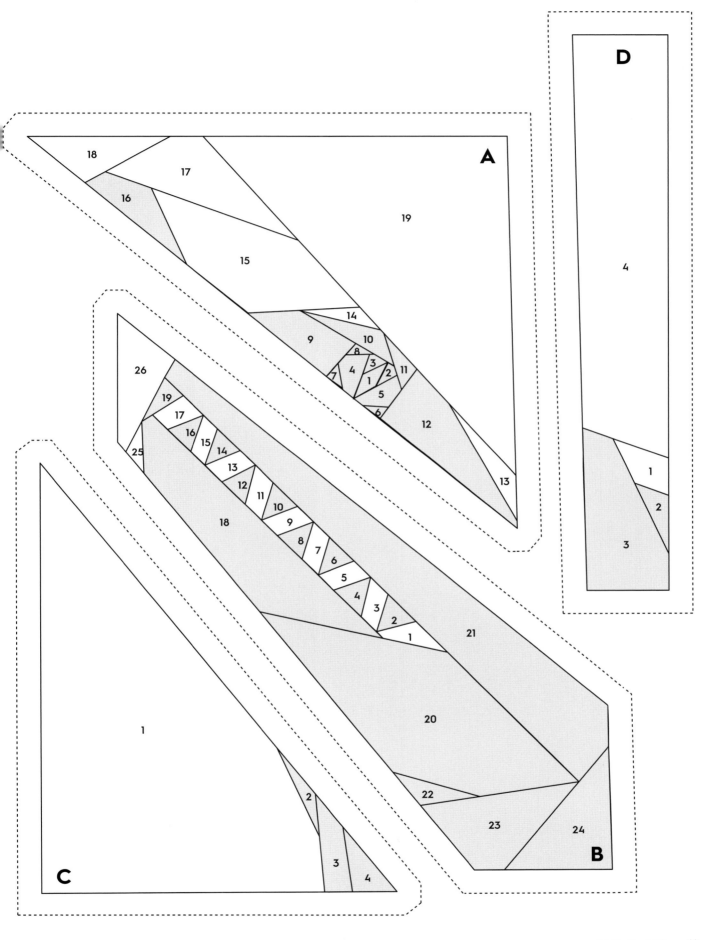

DRAGONFLY

Lindsay Chieco

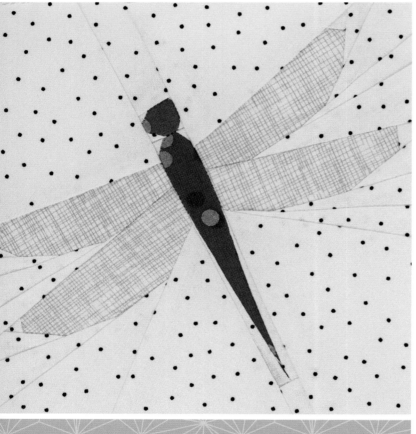

YOU WILL NEED

* Large scrap of white/light print fabric, at least 11" x 11" (28cm x 28cm)
* Smaller scraps of blue and grey fabrics

BLOCK CONSTRUCTION

Make one copy each of patterns A, B, C, D, E and F.

Complete sections A to F.

Join A to B. Press seam open.

Join C to D. Press seam towards D.

Join E to F. Press seam towards F.

Join CD to AB. Press seam towards CD.

Join CDAB to EF. Press seam towards EF.

REFERENCE DIAGRAM

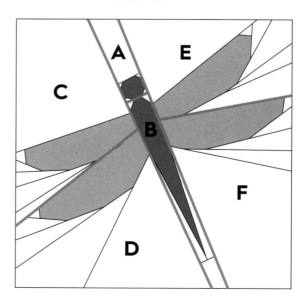

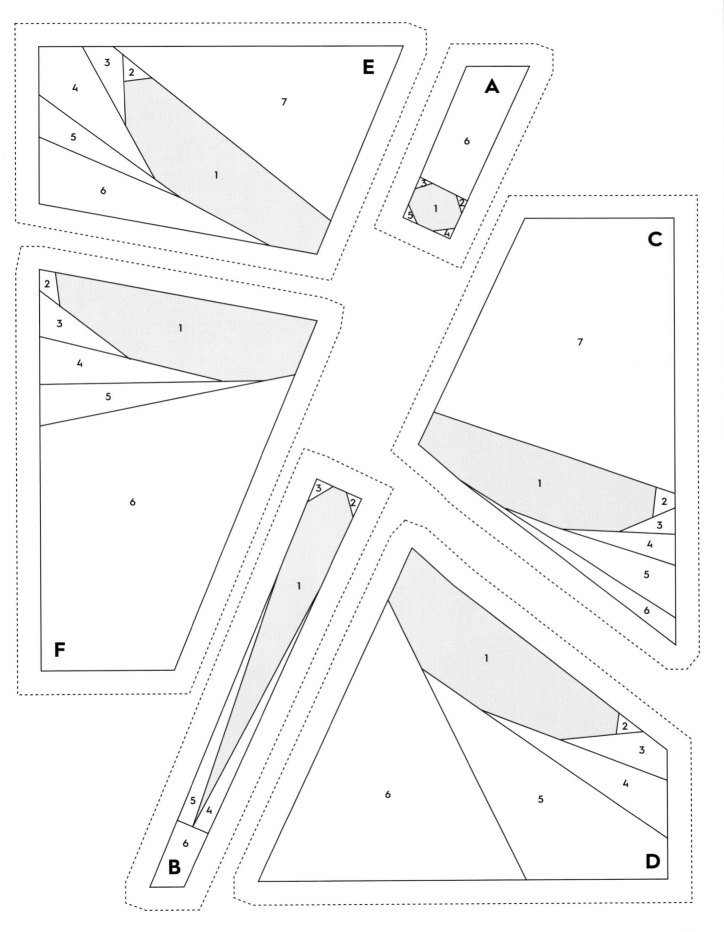

BUTTERFLY

Lindsay Chieco

YOU WILL NEED

* Large scrap of white/light print fabric, at least 11" x 11" (28cm x 28cm)
* Large scrap of blue fabric, at least 6" x 6" (15.5cm x 15.5cm)
* Smaller scrap of black fabric

BLOCK CONSTRUCTION

Make one copy each of patterns A, B, C, D, E, F and G.

Complete sections A to G.

Join A to B. Press seam open.

Join AB to C. Press seam open.

Join D to E. Press seam towards D.

Join F to G. Press seam towards F.

Join FG to ABC. Press seam towards FG.

Join DE to FGABC. Press seam towards DE.

REFERENCE DIAGRAM

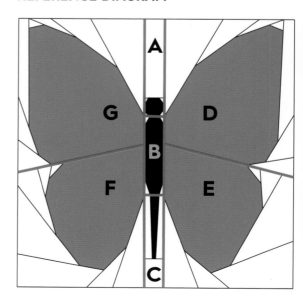

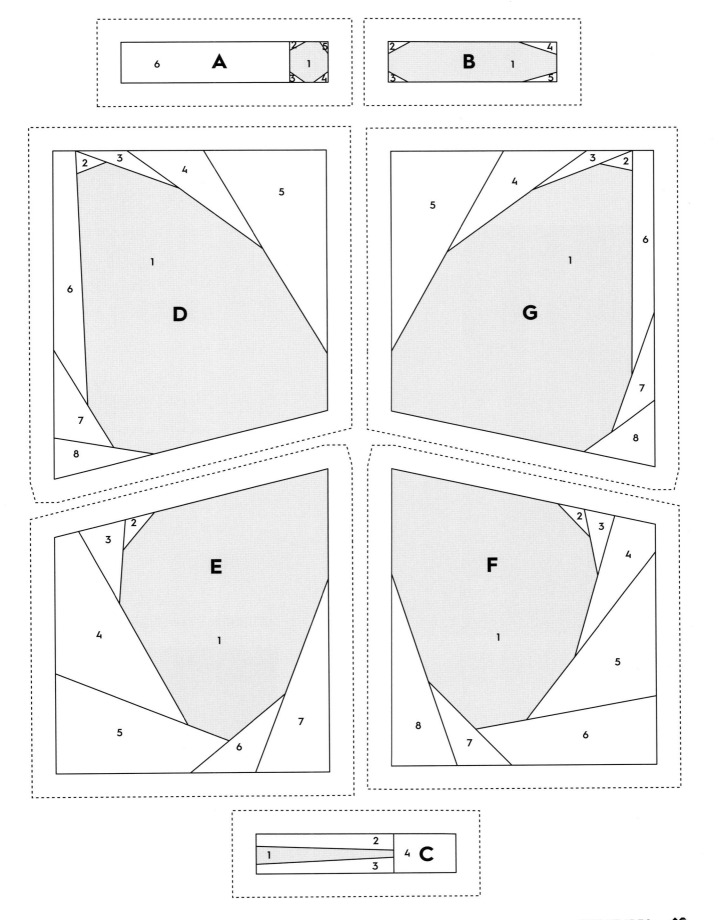

OWL
Juliet van der Heijden

YOU WILL NEED

- Large scrap of dark teal blue fabric, at least 12" x 12" (30.5cm x 30.5cm)
- Large scrap of light orange fabric, at least 10" x 10" (25.5cm x 25.5cm)
- Large scrap of burnt orange fabric, at least 10" x 10" (25.5cm x 25.5cm)
- Large scrap of caramel fabric, at least 8" x 6" (20.5cm x 15.5cm)
- Smaller scraps of black, yellow and bright orange fabrics

BLOCK CONSTRUCTION

Make one copy each of patterns A, B, C and D.

Complete sections A to D.

Join A to B. Press seam open.

Join C to D. Press seam open.

Join AB to CD. Press seam open.

REFERENCE DIAGRAM

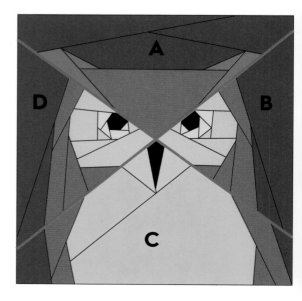

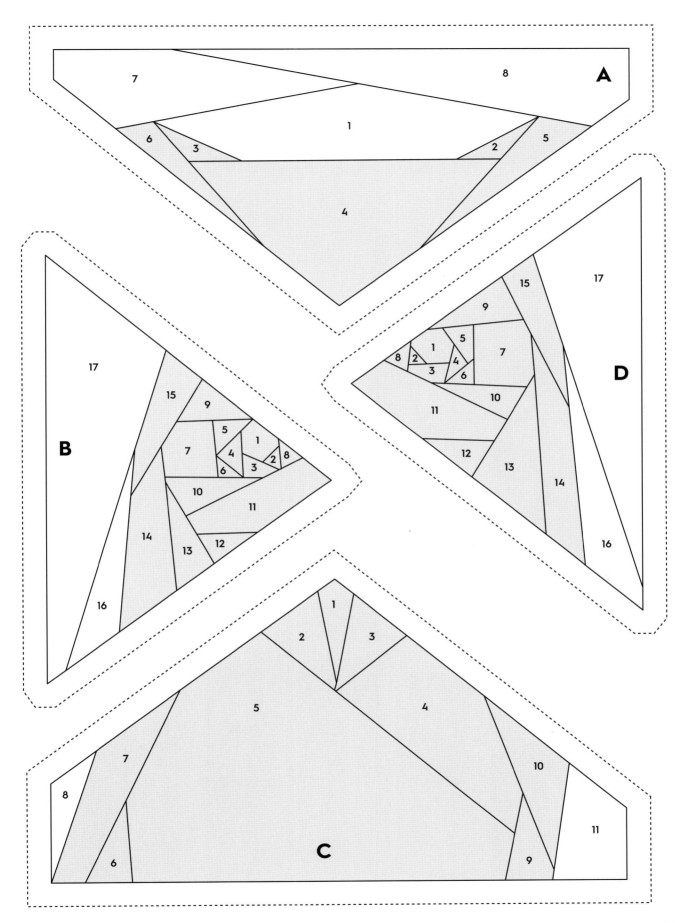

GOLDFISH
Jo Carter

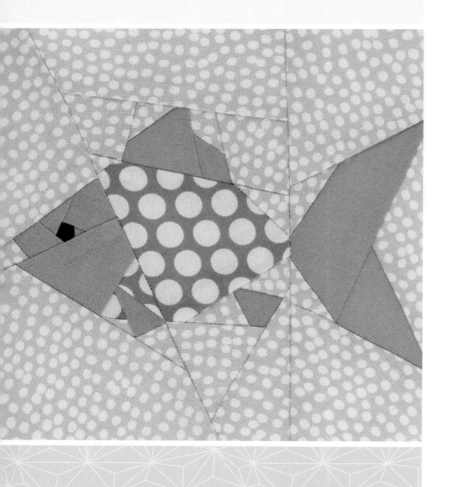

YOU WILL NEED

* Large scrap of pale blue fabric, at least 11" x 11" (28cm x 28cm)
* Large scrap of orange fabric, at least 7" x 7" (18cm x 18cm)
* Smaller scraps of black and orange print fabric

BLOCK CONSTRUCTION

Make one copy each of patterns A, B, C, D and E.

Complete sections A to E.

Join A to B. Press seam towards B.

Join C to D. Press seam towards D.

Join AB to CD. Press seam towards CD.

Join ABCD to E. Press seam towards E.

REFERENCE DIAGRAM

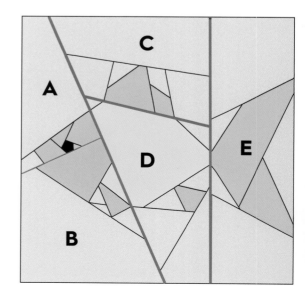

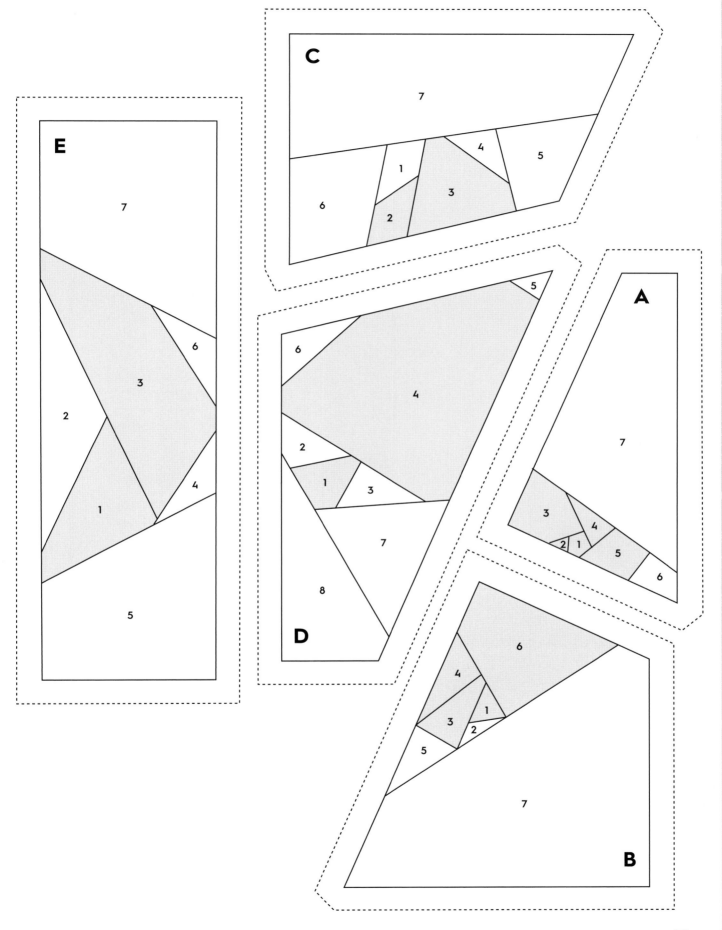

FROG

Juliet van der Heijden

YOU WILL NEED

* One fat eighth of magenta fabric
* Large scrap of dark green fabric, at least 9" x 9" (23cm x 23cm)
* Large scrap of mid green fabric, at least 6½" x 1½" (16.5cm x 4cm)
* Large scrap of lime green fabric, at least 6" x 4" (15.5cm x 10cm)
* Smaller scraps of black and yellow fabrics

BLOCK CONSTRUCTION

Make one copy each of patterns A, B, C, D and E.

Complete sections A to E.

Join A to B. Press seam open

Join AB to C. Press seam open.

Join D to E. Press seam open.

Join ABC to DE. Press seam open.

REFERENCE DIAGRAM

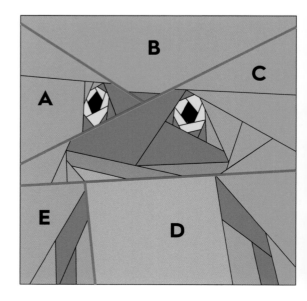

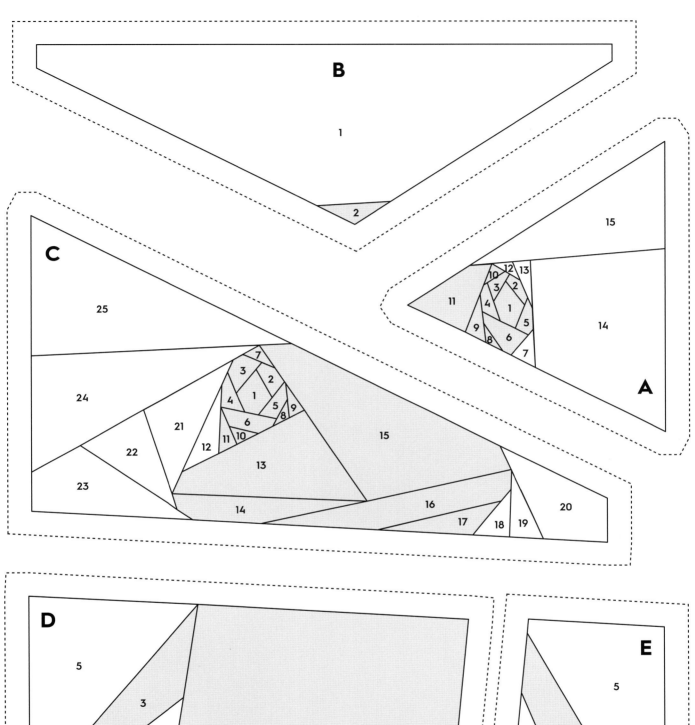

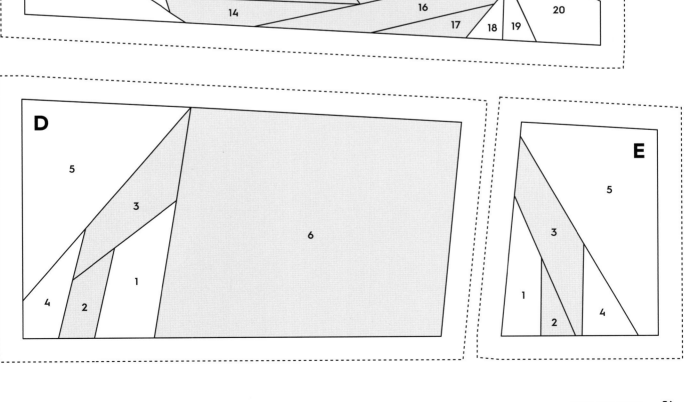

PUFFIN

Juliet van der Heijden

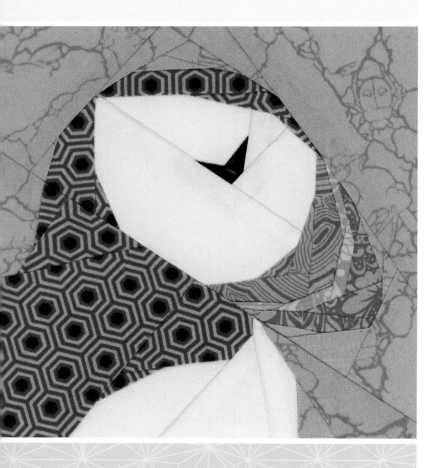

YOU WILL NEED

- Large scrap of light green fabric, at least 10" x 14" (25.5cm x 35.5cm)
- Large scrap of white fabric, at least 12" x 12" (30.5cm x 30.5cm)
- Large scrap of dark blue fabric, at least 10" x 10" (25.5cm x 25.5cm)
- Smaller scraps of black, light blue, yellow and pink fabrics

BLOCK CONSTRUCTION

Make one copy each of patterns A, B and C.

Complete sections A to C.

Join A to B. Press seam open.

Join AB to C. Press seam open.

REFERENCE DIAGRAM

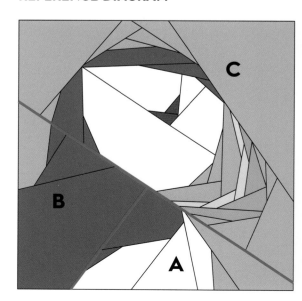

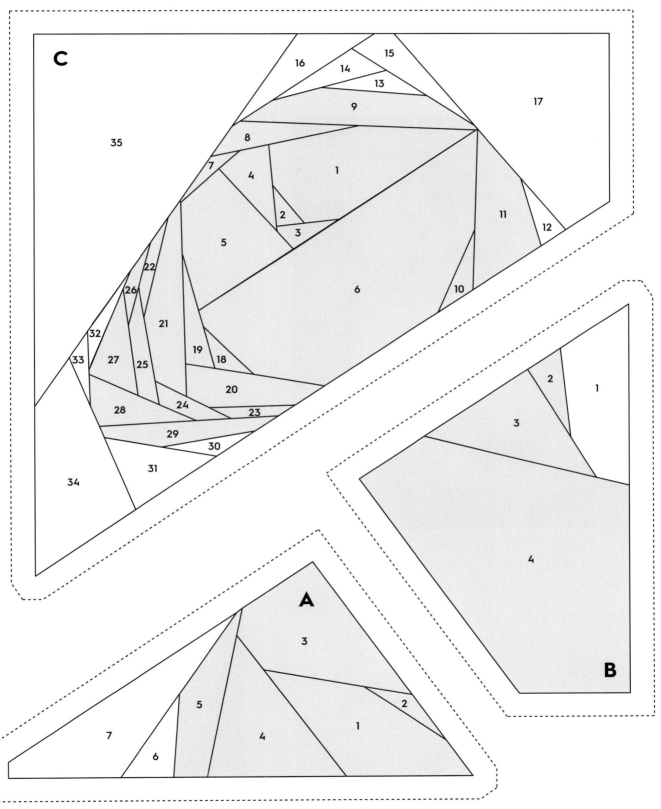

RACCOON

Juliet van der Heijden

YOU WILL NEED

- One fat eighth of blue fabric
- Large scrap of light grey fabric, at least 11" x 11" (28cm x 28cm)
- Smaller scraps of black, pink, white and dark grey fabrics

BLOCK CONSTRUCTION

Make one copy each of patterns A, B, C, D and E.

Complete sections A to E.

Join A to B. Press seam open.

Join C to D. Press seam open.

Join AB to CD. Press seam open.

Join ABCD to E. Press seam open.

REFERENCE DIAGRAM

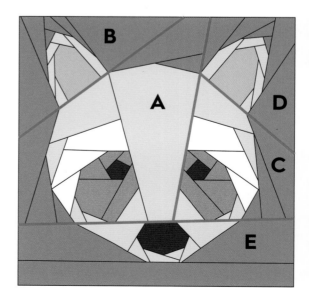

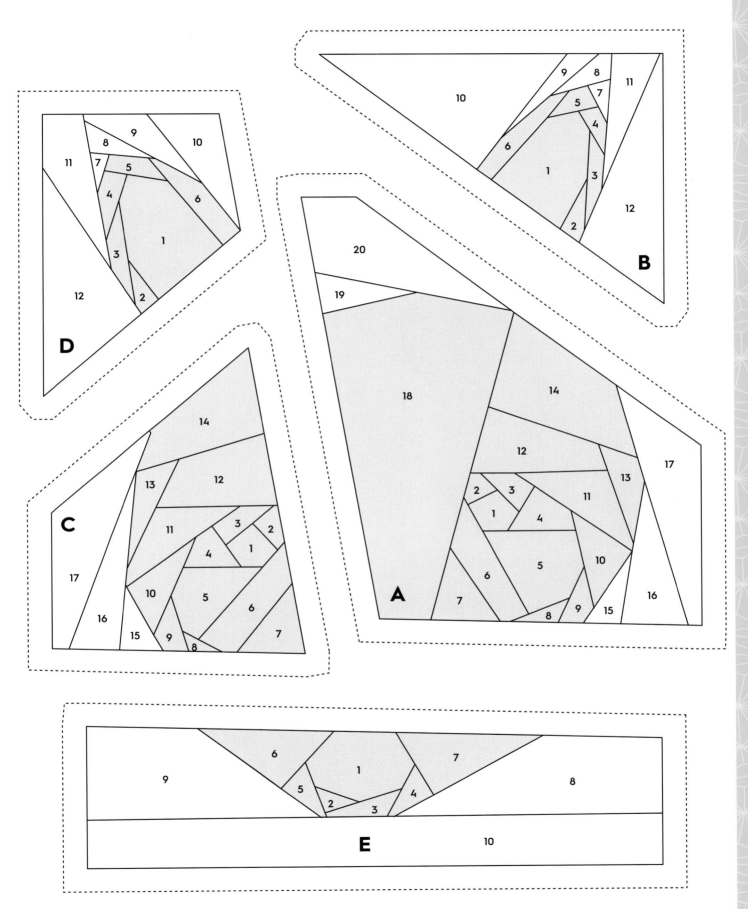

LADYBIRD
Kristy Lea

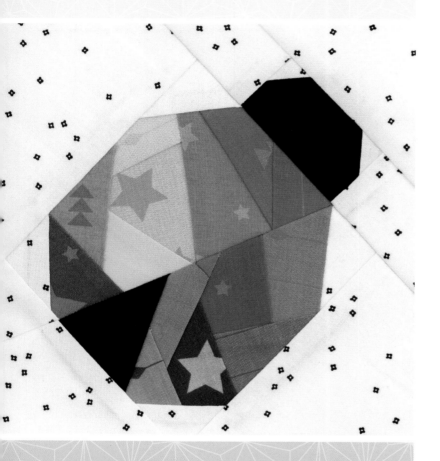

YOU WILL NEED

- One fat eighth of white/light print fabric
- Smaller scraps of rainbow shades and black fabrics

BLOCK CONSTRUCTION

Make one copy each of patterns A, B and C.

Complete sections A to C.

Join A to B. Press seam towards B.

Join AB to C. Press seam towards C.

REFERENCE DIAGRAM

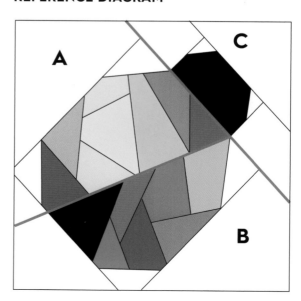

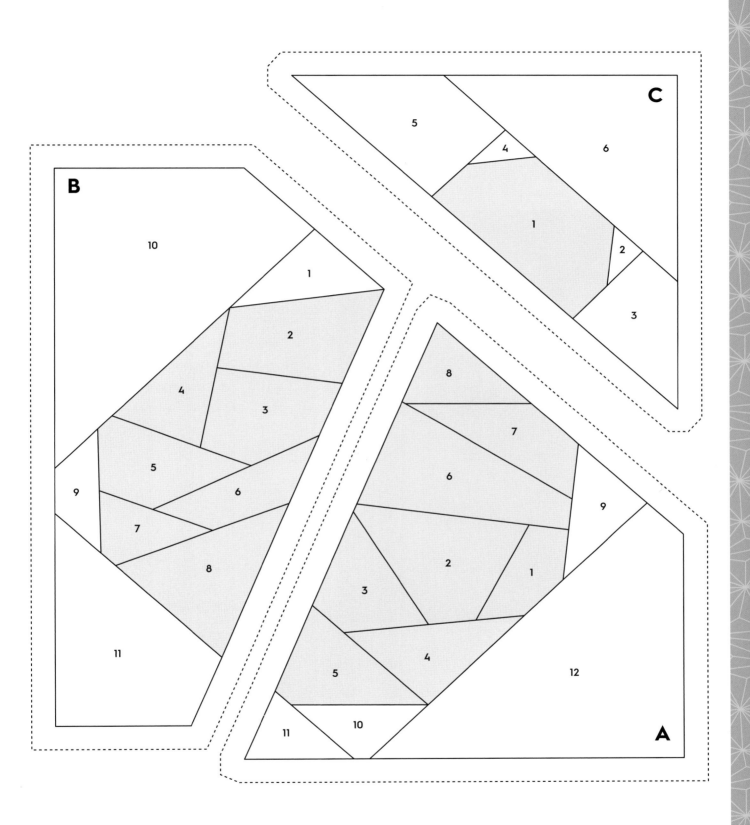

FIREFLY

Lindsay Chieco

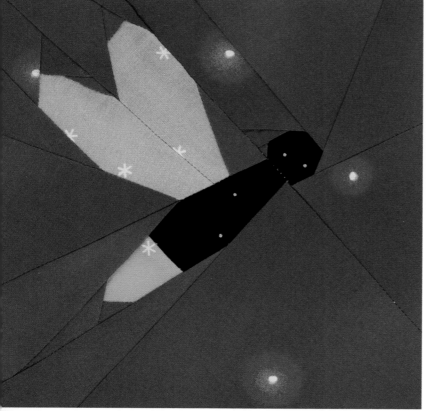

YOU WILL NEED

* Large scrap of blue fabric, at least 11" x 11" (28cm x 28cm)
* Smaller scraps of black, yellow and grey fabrics

BLOCK CONSTRUCTION

Make one copy each of patterns A, B, C and D.

Complete sections A to D.

Join C to D. Press seam towards D.

Join CD to A. Press seam towards A.

Join CDA to B. Press seam towards CDA.

REFERENCE DIAGRAM

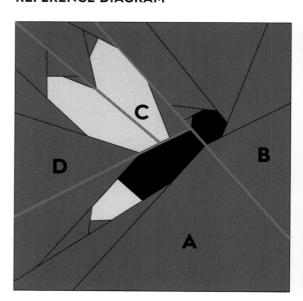

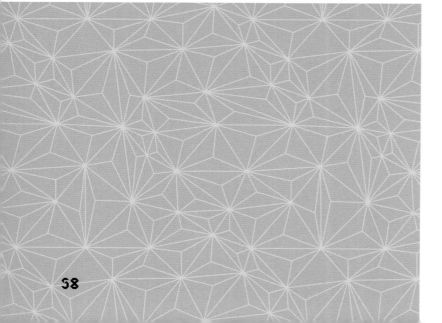

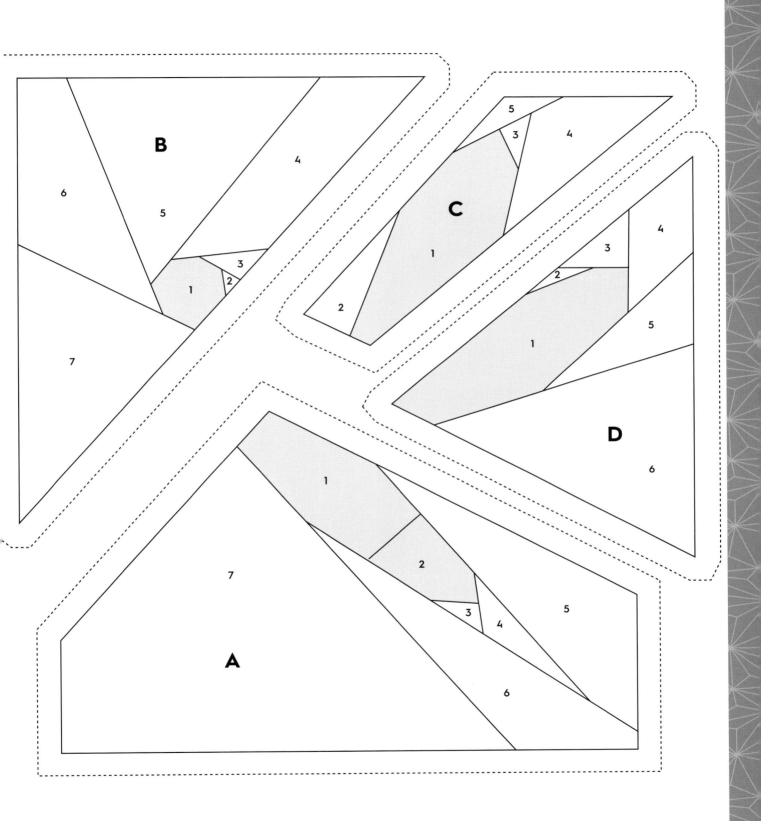

BURGER

Joanne Hart

YOU WILL NEED

- One fat eighth of white/light print fabric
- Large scrap of tan fabric, at least 10" x 10" (25.5cm x 25.5cm)
- Smaller scraps of brown, yellow, yellow-green and bright pink fabrics

BLOCK CONSTRUCTION

Make one copy each of patterns A, B and C.

Complete sections A to C.

Join A to B. Press seam towards B.

Join AB to C. Press seam towards C.

REFERENCE DIAGRAM

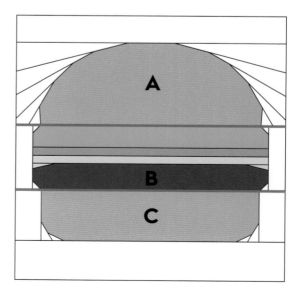

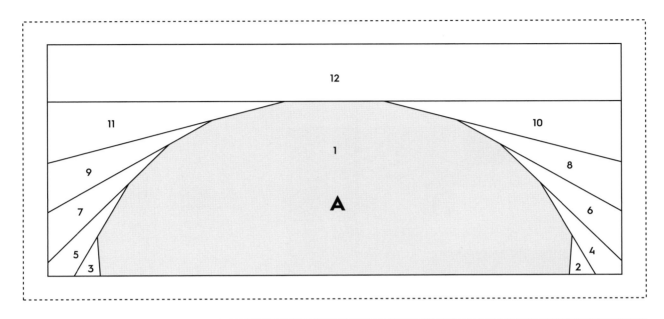

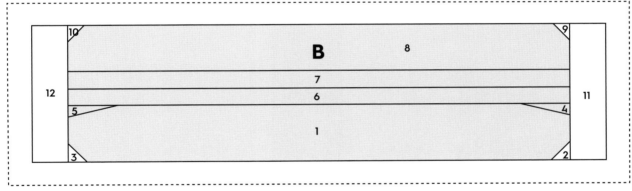

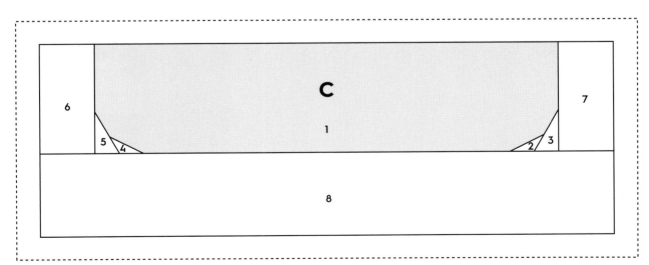

MILKSHAKE

Lindsay Chieco

YOU WILL NEED

* Large scrap of blue fabric, at least 11" x 11" (28cm x 28cm)
* Smaller scraps of brown, grey, white, red and red and white stripe fabrics

BLOCK CONSTRUCTION

Make one copy each of patterns A, B, C, D, E, F and G.

Complete sections A to G.

Join C to D. Press seam open.

Join CD to E. Press seam open.

Join CDE to F. Press seam towards F.

Join CDEF to G. Press seam towards G.

Join CDEFG to B. Press seam towards B.

Join CDEFGB to A. Press seam towards A.

REFERENCE DIAGRAM

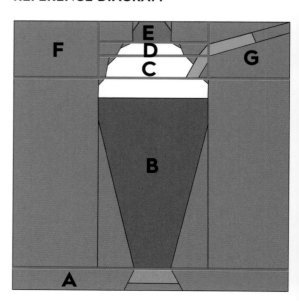

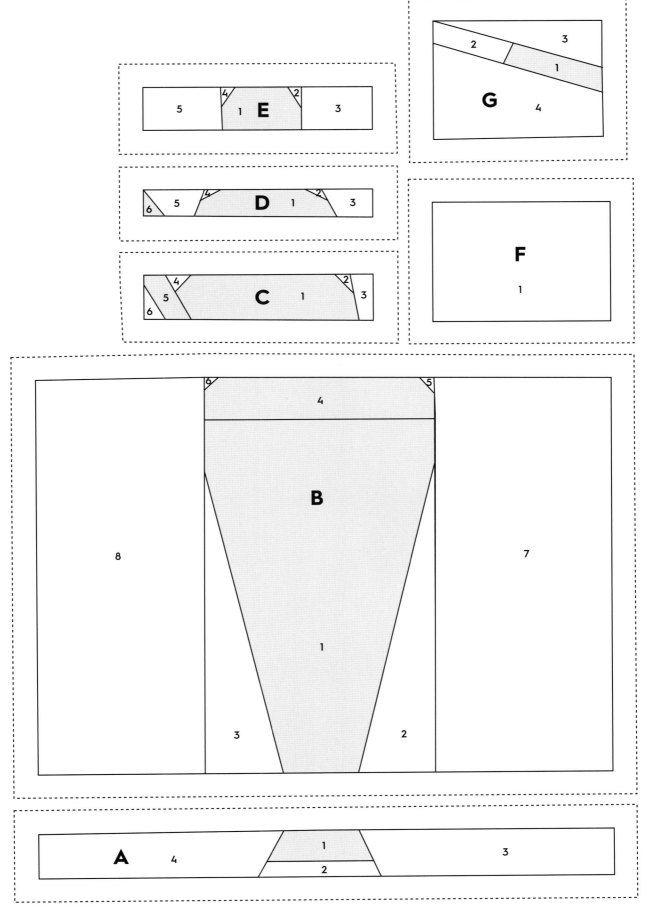

PRETZEL

Monika Henry

YOU WILL NEED

* Large scrap of white fabric, at least 3½"
  x 15" (9cm x 38cm)
* Large scrap of brown fabric, at least
  7½" x 15" (19cm x 38cm)

BLOCK CONSTRUCTION

Make one copy each of patterns A, B, C,
D, E and F.

Complete sections A to F.

Join A to B. Press seam towards A.

Join AB to C. Press seam towards C.

Join D to E. Press seam towards D.

Join DE to F. Press seam towards DE.

Join ABC to DEF, nesting the seams. Press
seam open.

REFERENCE DIAGRAM

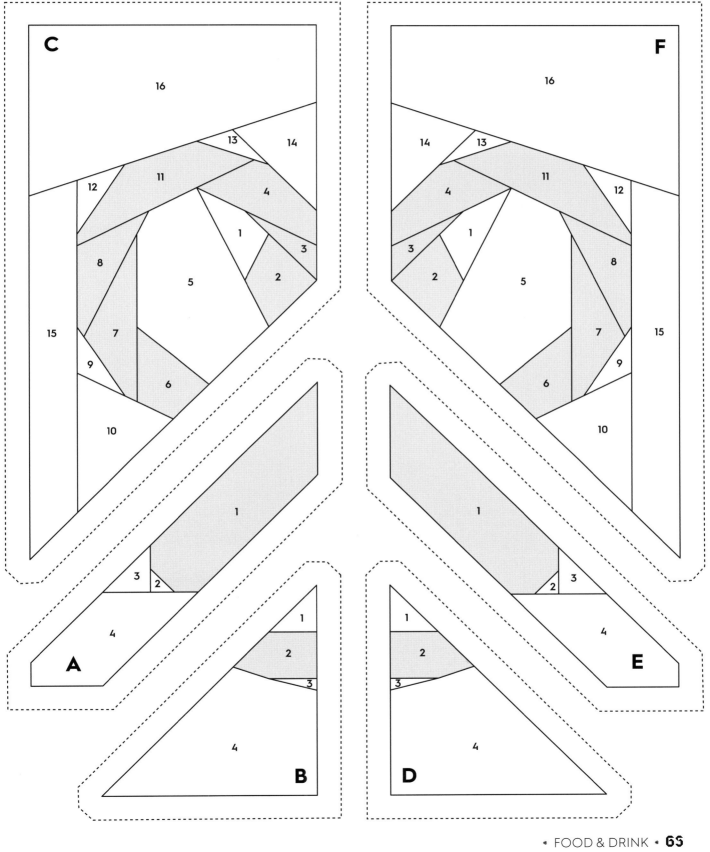

PIZZA SLICE

Joanne Hart

YOU WILL NEED

- One fat eighth of white/light print fabric
- One fat eighth of beige fabric
- Smaller scraps of bright pink and brown fabrics

BLOCK CONSTRUCTION

Make one copy each of patterns A, B, C, D, E and F.

Complete sections A to F.

Join A to B. Press seam towards A.

Join AB to C. Press seam towards AB.

Join ABC to D. Press seam towards D.

Join ABCD to E. Press seams towards E.

Join ABCDE to F. Press seam towards F.

REFERENCE DIAGRAM

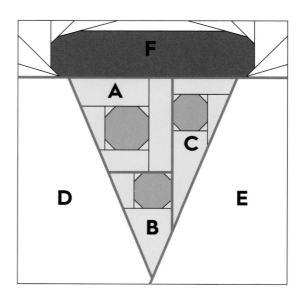

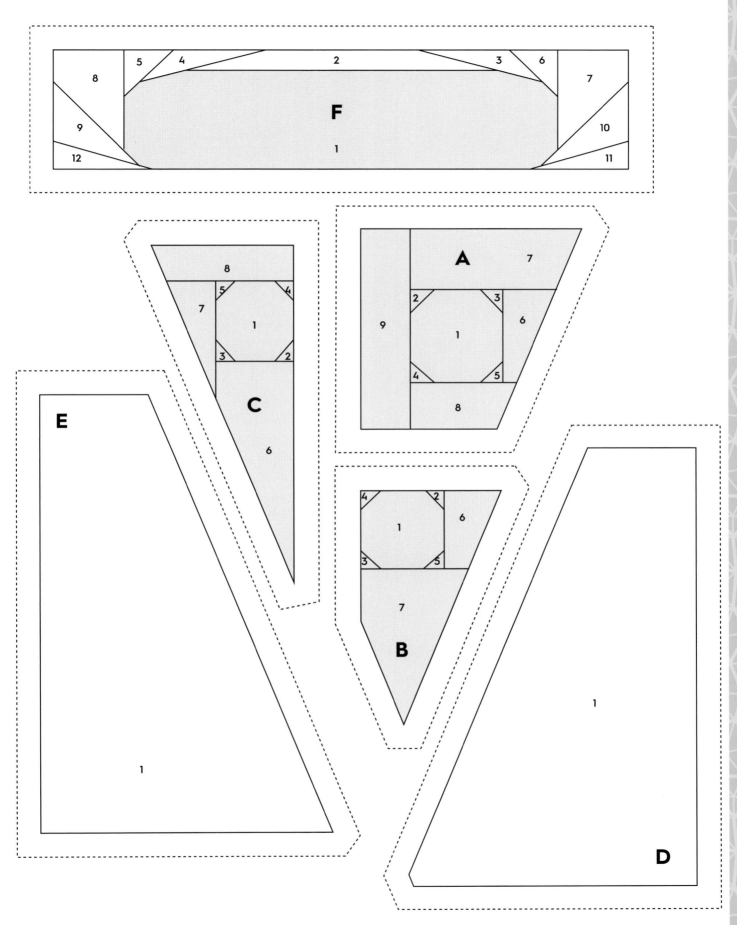

LEMONADE

Lindsay Chieco

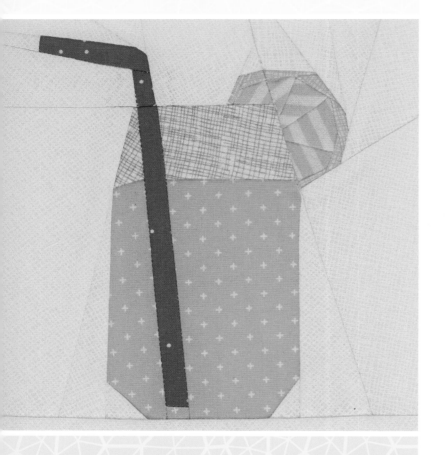

YOU WILL NEED

- Large scrap of white fabric, at least 11" x 11" (28cm x 28cm)
- Smaller scraps of light yellow, mid yellow, yellow and white stripe, grey print, and pink fabrics

BLOCK CONSTRUCTION

Make one copy each of patterns A, B, C, D, E and F.

Complete sections A to F.

Join B to C. Press seam towards C.

Join E to D. Press seam towards D.

Join BC to ED. Press seam towards BC.

Join A to BCED. Press seam towards BCED.

Join F to ABCED. Press seam towards ABCED.

REFERENCE DIAGRAM

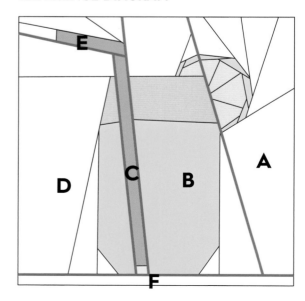

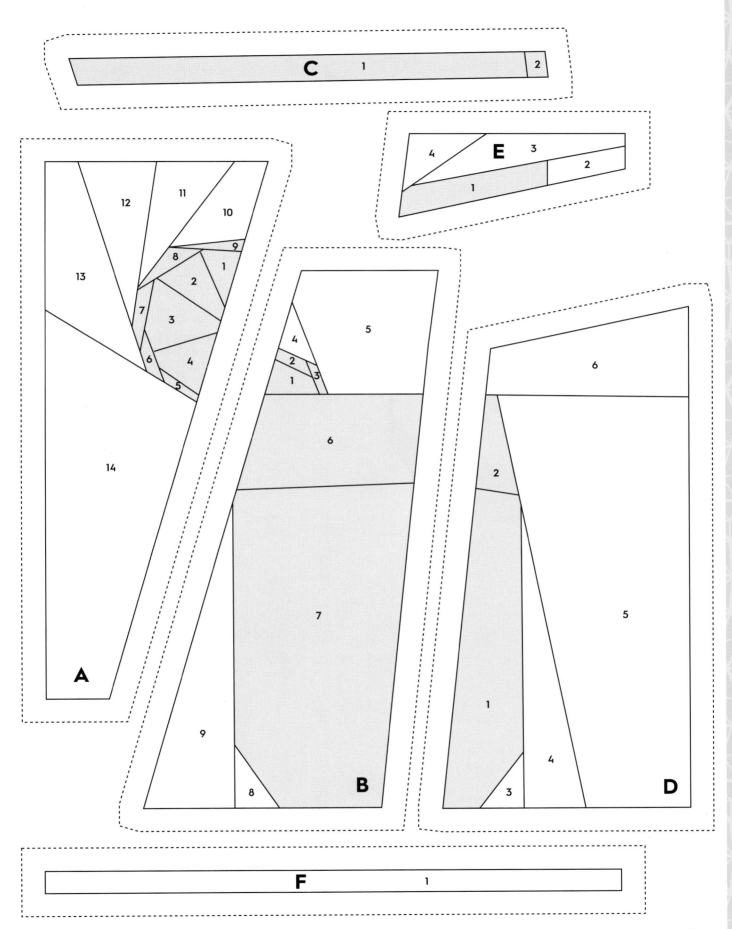

DOUGHNUT

Monika Henry

YOU WILL NEED

* Large scrap of white fabric, at least 7" x 12" (18cm x 30.5cm)
* Large scrap of white sprinkle print fabric, at least 5" x 7" (13cm x 18cm)
* Large scrap of dark brown fabric, at least 5" x 6" (13cm x 15.5cm)

BLOCK CONSTRUCTION

Make one copy of pattern A.

Complete section A.

REFERENCE DIAGRAM

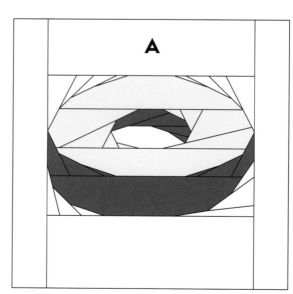

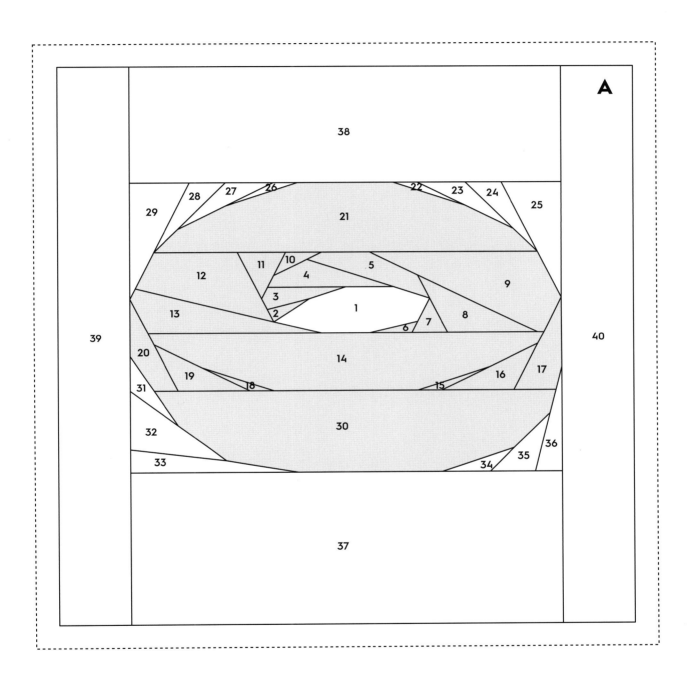

ICE CREAM

Lindsay Chieco

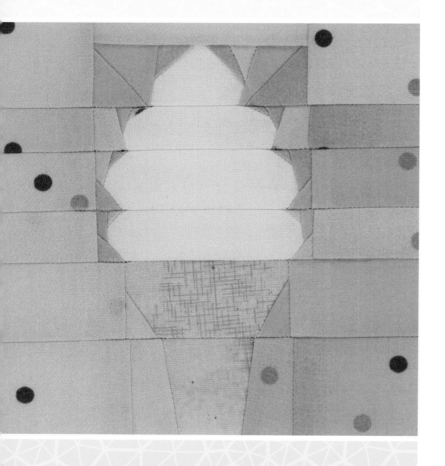

YOU WILL NEED

- Large scrap of green fabric, at least 11" x 11" (28cm x 28cm)
- Smaller scraps of white and tan fabrics

BLOCK CONSTRUCTION

Make one copy each of patterns A, B, C, D, E and F.

Complete sections A to F.

Join A to B. Press seam towards A.

Join AB to C. Press seam towards AB.

Join ABC to D. Press seam towards ABC.

Join ABCD to E. Press seam towards ABCD.

Join ABCDE to F. Press seam towards ABCDE.

REFERENCE DIAGRAM

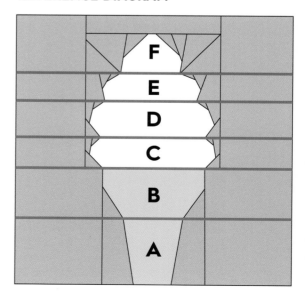

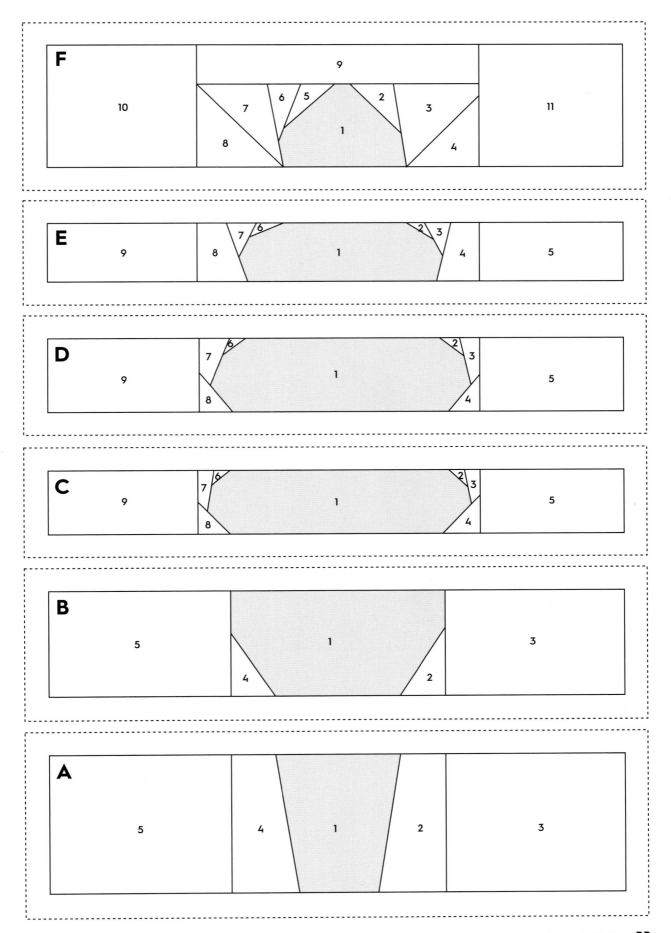

POPCORN

Monika Henry

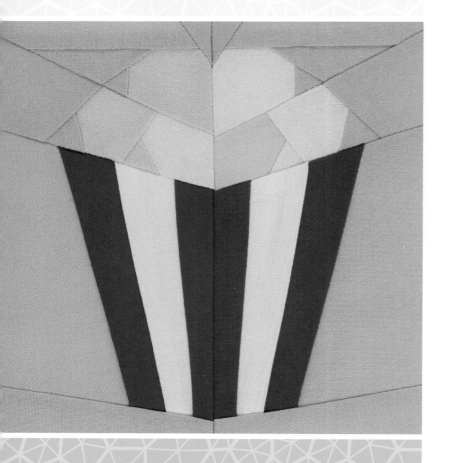

YOU WILL NEED

* Large scrap of light blue fabric, at least 5" x 18" (13cm x 45.5cm)

* Large scrap of mink fabric, at least 2" x 7" (5cm x 18cm)

* Large scrap of ivory fabric, at least 2" x 7" (5cm x 18cm)

* Smaller scraps of red and white fabrics

BLOCK CONSTRUCTION

Make one copy each of patterns A, B, C, D, E and F.

Complete sections A to F.

Join C to B. Press seam towards B.

Join BC to A. Press seam towards A.

Join F to E. Press seam towards F.

Join EF to D. Press seam towards EF.

Join ABC to DEF, nesting the seams. Press seam open.

REFERENCE DIAGRAM

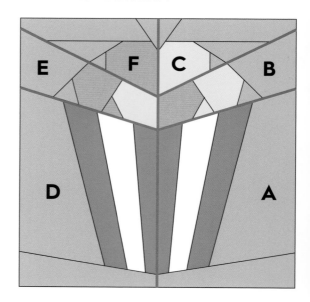

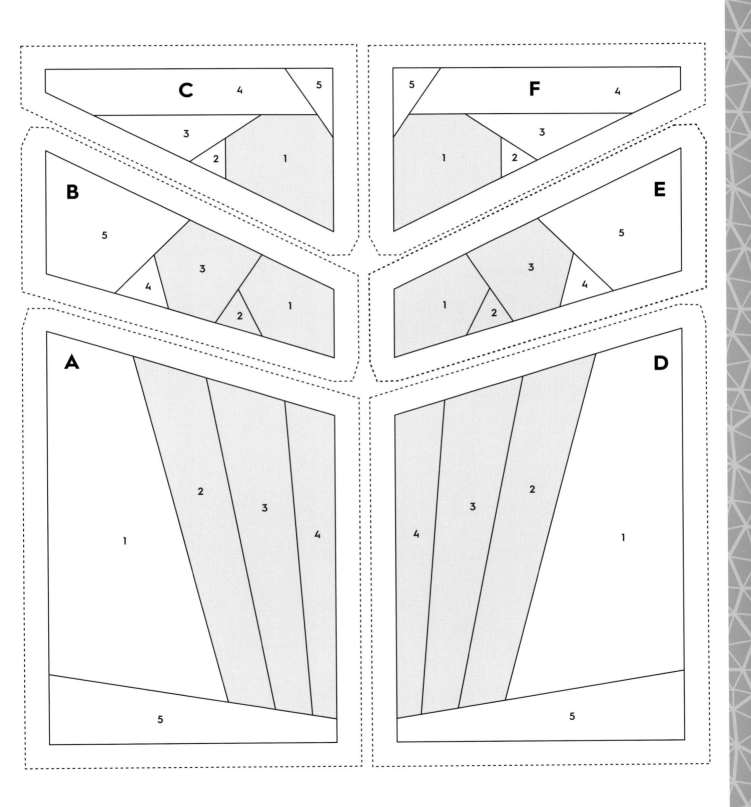

PIE
Susan White

YOU WILL NEED

* One fat eighth of white fabric
* Smaller scraps of gold, navy blue and mink fabrics

BLOCK CONSTRUCTION

Make one copy each of patterns A and B.

Complete sections A and B.

Join A to B. Press seam towards A.

REFERENCE DIAGRAM

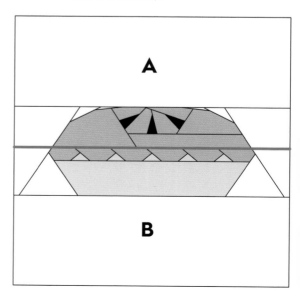

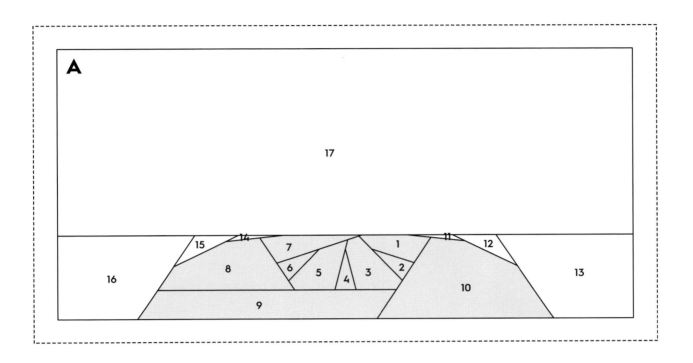

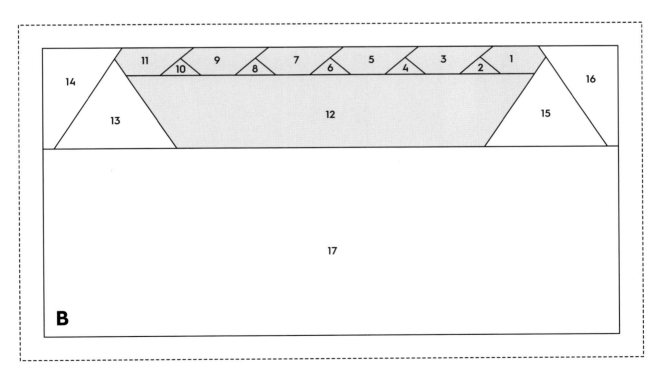

LOLLIPOP

Monika Henry

YOU WILL NEED

- Large scrap of white fabric, at least 6" x 12" (15.5cm x 30.5cm)
- Large scraps of yellow and orange fabric, each at least 2½" x 14" (6.5cm x 35.5cm)
- Smaller scrap of brown fabric

BLOCK CONSTRUCTION

Make one copy each of patterns A, B, C, D, E, F, G, H and I.

Complete sections A to I.

Join A to B. Press seam open.

Join C to D. Press seam open.

Join E to F. Press seam open.

Join G to H. Press seam open.

Join AB to CD. Press seam towards AB.

Join EF to GH. Press seam towards EF.

Join ABCD to EFGH, nesting the seams. Press seam open.

Join ABCDEFGH to I. Press seam towards I.

REFERENCE DIAGRAM

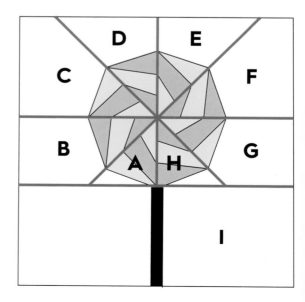

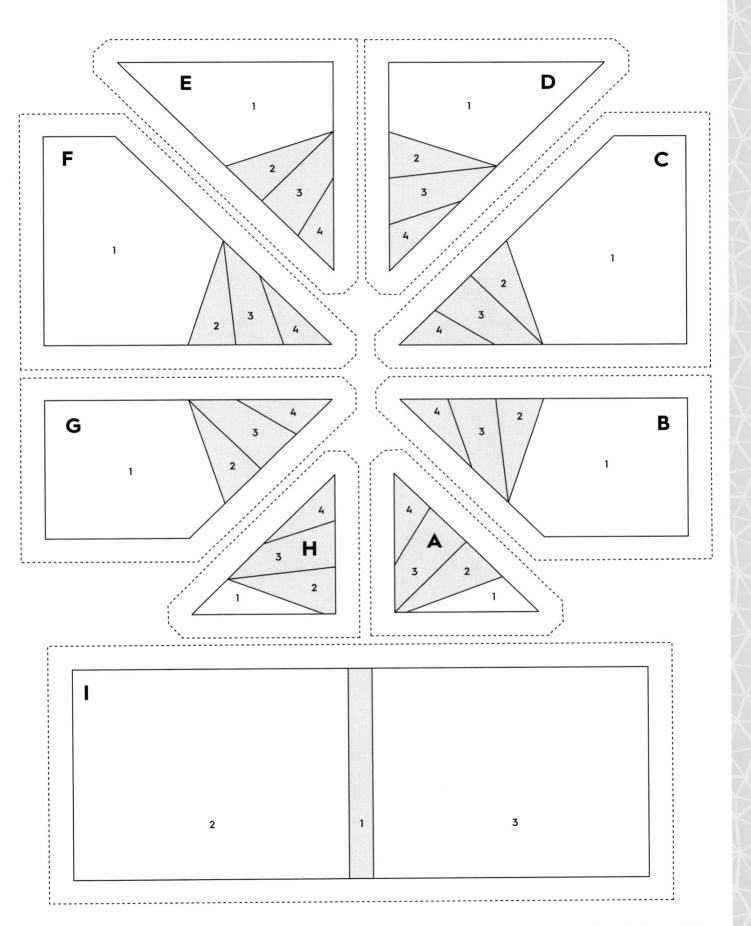

COCKTAIL

Sarah Ashford

YOU WILL NEED

- Large scrap of lime fabric, at least 9" x 8" (23cm x 20.5cm)
- Smaller scraps of dark pink, light pink and black fabrics
- Small pink button

BLOCK CONSTRUCTION

Make one copy each of patterns A, B, C and D.

Complete sections A to D.

Join A to B. Press seam towards A.

Join C to D. Press seam towards C.

Join AB to CD. Press seam towards AB.

Sew the button decoration onto the top edge of the glass.

REFERENCE DIAGRAM

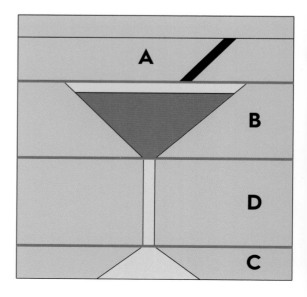

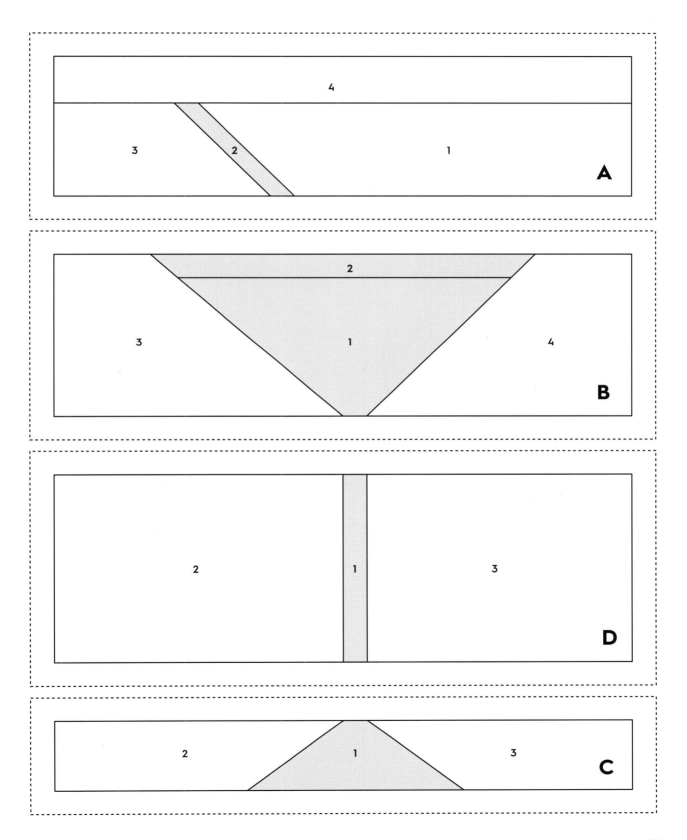

AVOCADO

Monika Henry

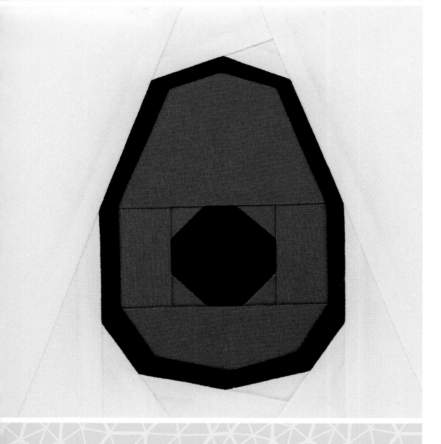

YOU WILL NEED

- Large scrap of white fabric, at least 7" x 10" (18cm x 25.5cm)
- Large scrap of light green fabric, at least 3½" x 10" (9cm x 25.5cm)
- Large scrap of dark green fabric, at least 3½" x 10" (9cm x 25.5cm)
- Smaller scrap of brown fabric

BLOCK CONSTRUCTION

Make one copy of pattern A.

Complete section A.

REFERENCE DIAGRAM

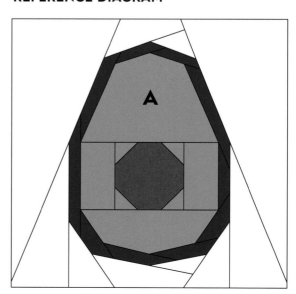

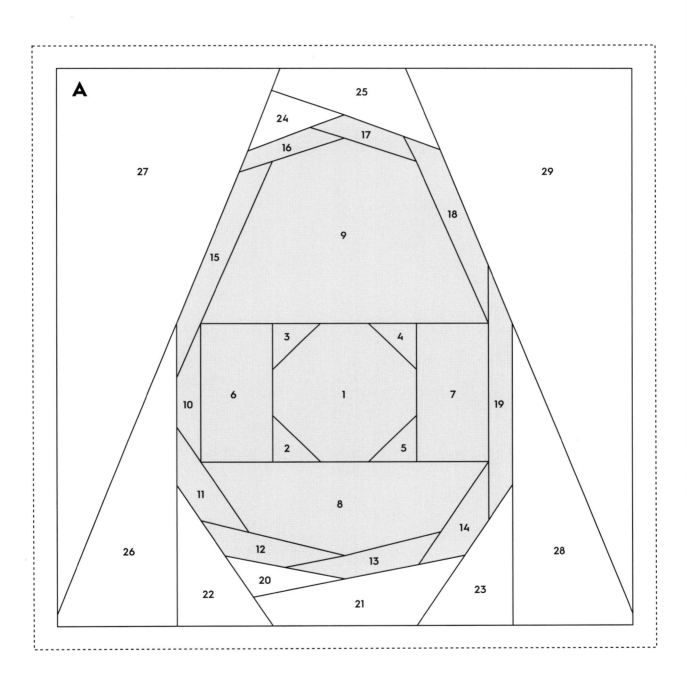

SMOOTHIE

Joanne Hart

YOU WILL NEED

* One fat eighth of white/light print fabric
* Large scrap of pink fabric, 10" x 10" (25.5cm x 25.5cm)
* Smaller scraps of pink strawberry print and black and white stripe fabrics

BLOCK CONSTRUCTION

Make one copy each of patterns A, B, C, D and E.

Complete sections A to E.

Join A to B. Press seam towards A.

Join AB to C. Press seam towards AB.

Join ABC to D. Press seam towards D.

Join ABCD to E. Press seam towards E.

REFERENCE DIAGRAM

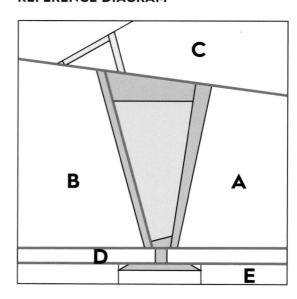

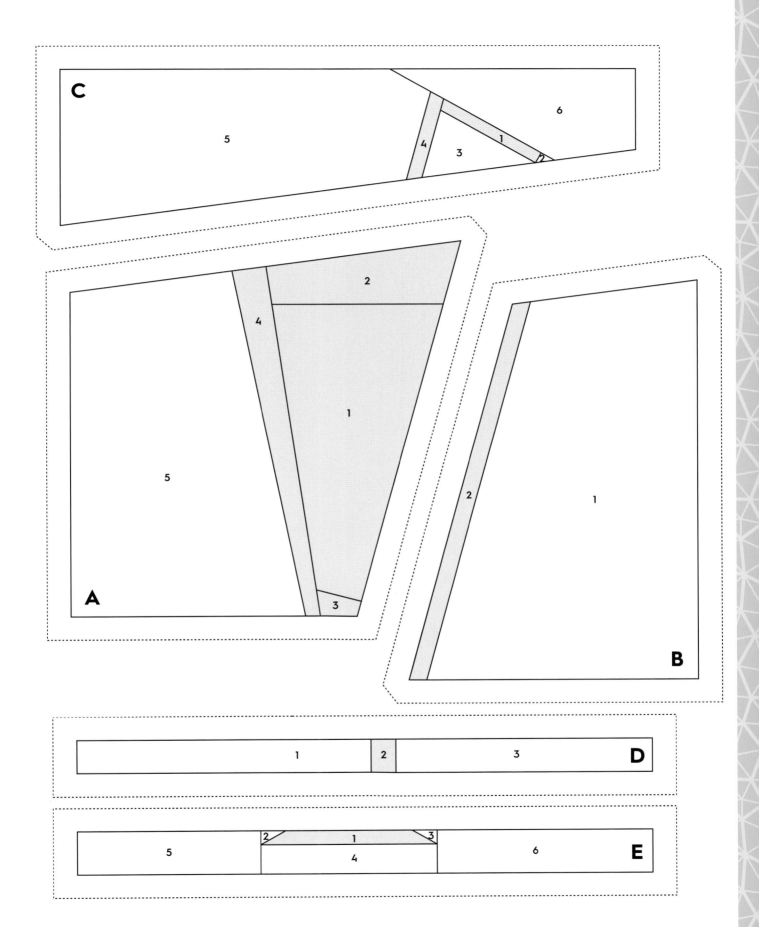

POPSICLE

Lindsay Chieco

YOU WILL NEED

* Large scrap of blue fabric, at least 11" x 11" (28cm x 28cm)
* Smaller scraps of pink and tan fabrics

BLOCK CONSTRUCTION

Make one copy each of patterns A and B.

Complete sections A to B.

Join A to B. Press seam towards B.

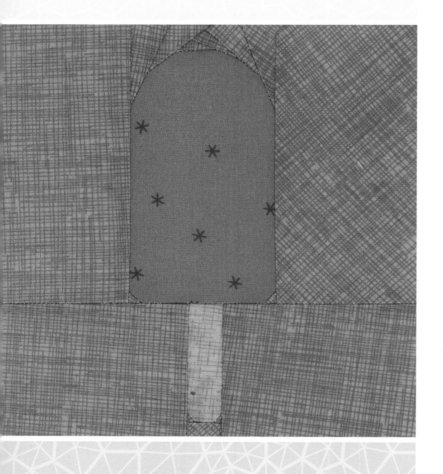

REFERENCE DIAGRAM

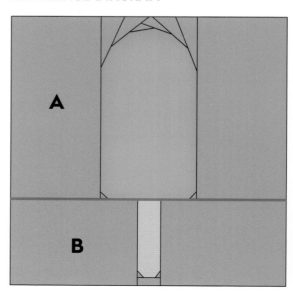

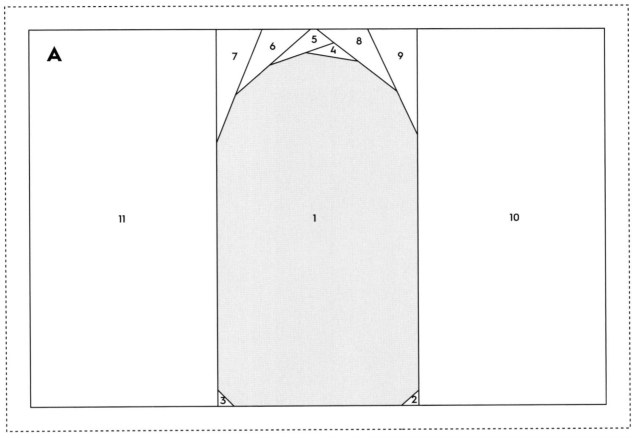

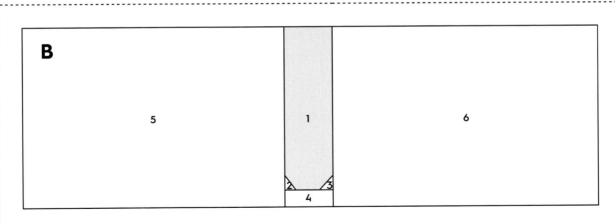

SUN
Kerry Green

YOU WILL NEED

* Large scrap of blue fabric, at least 13" x 13" (33cm x 33cm)
* Large scrap of dark yellow fabric, at least 10" x 12" (25.5cm x 30.5cm)
* Large scrap of light yellow fabric, at least 2½" x 11" (6.5cm x 11cm)

BLOCK CONSTRUCTION

Make one copy each of patterns A, B and C.

Complete sections A to C.

Join A to B. Press seam open.

Join AB to C. Press seam open.

REFERENCE DIAGRAM

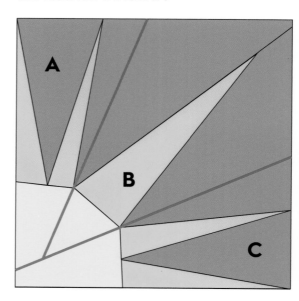

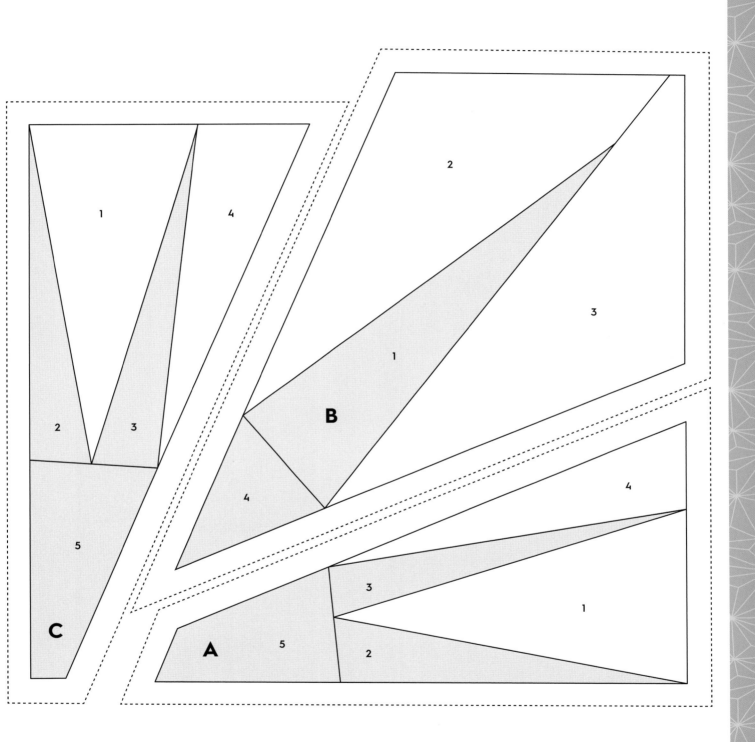

SUNGLASSES

Charise Randell

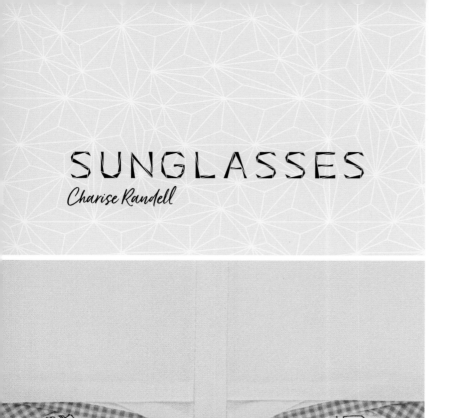

YOU WILL NEED

* One fat eighth of white fabric
* Large scrap of blue gingham fabric, at least 10" x 10" (25.5cm x 25.5cm)
* Large scrap of grey print fabric, at least 7" x 7" (18cm x 18cm)

BLOCK CONSTRUCTION

Make one copy each of patterns A, B and C.

Complete sections A to C.

Join A to B. Press seam towards B.

Join C to AB. Press seam towards AB.

REFERENCE DIAGRAM

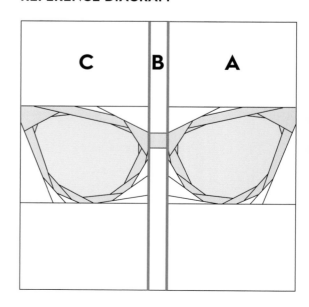

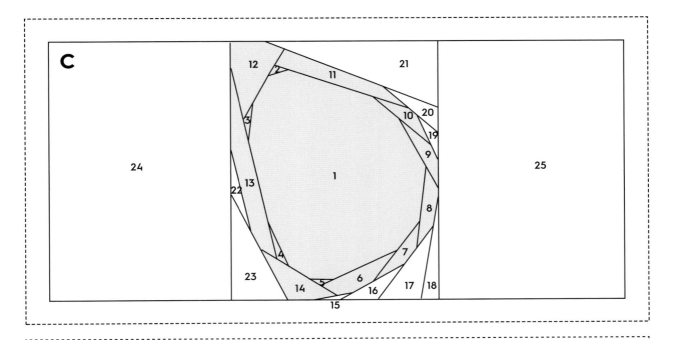

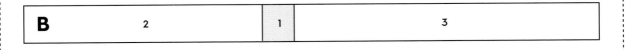

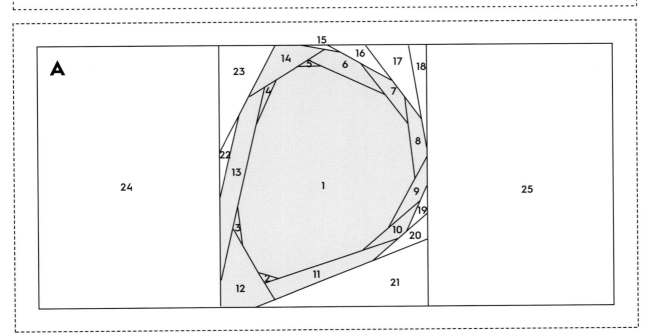

CLOUD

Susan White

YOU WILL NEED

- One fat eighth of blue fabric
- Smaller scrap of white fabric

BLOCK CONSTRUCTION

Make one copy each of patterns A, B and C.

Complete sections A to C.

Join A to B. Press seam towards A.

Join AB to C. Press seam towards C.

REFERENCE DIAGRAM

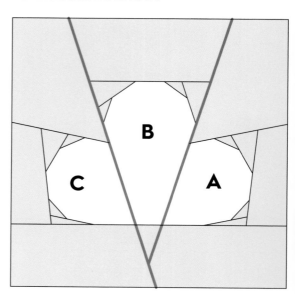

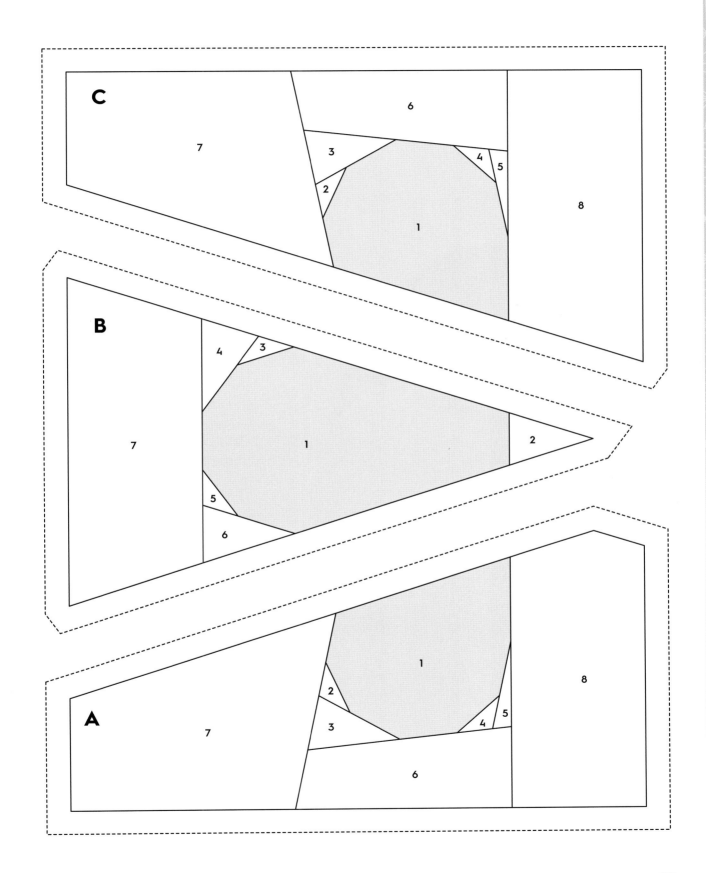

UMBRELLA

Lindsay Chieco

YOU WILL NEED

- Large scrap of white fabric, at least 11" x 11" (28cm x 28cm)
- Smaller scraps of blue, pink, purple and grey fabrics

BLOCK CONSTRUCTION

Make one copy each of patterns A, B, C, D, E, F and G.

Complete sections A to G.

Join A to B. Press seam towards B.

Join C to D. Press seam towards C.

Join CD to E. Press seam towards E.

Join F to G. Press seam towards G.

Join FG to CDE. Press seam towards CDE.

Join FGCDE to AB. Press seam towards AB.

REFERENCE DIAGRAM

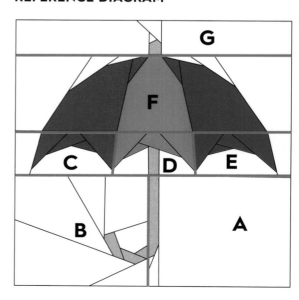

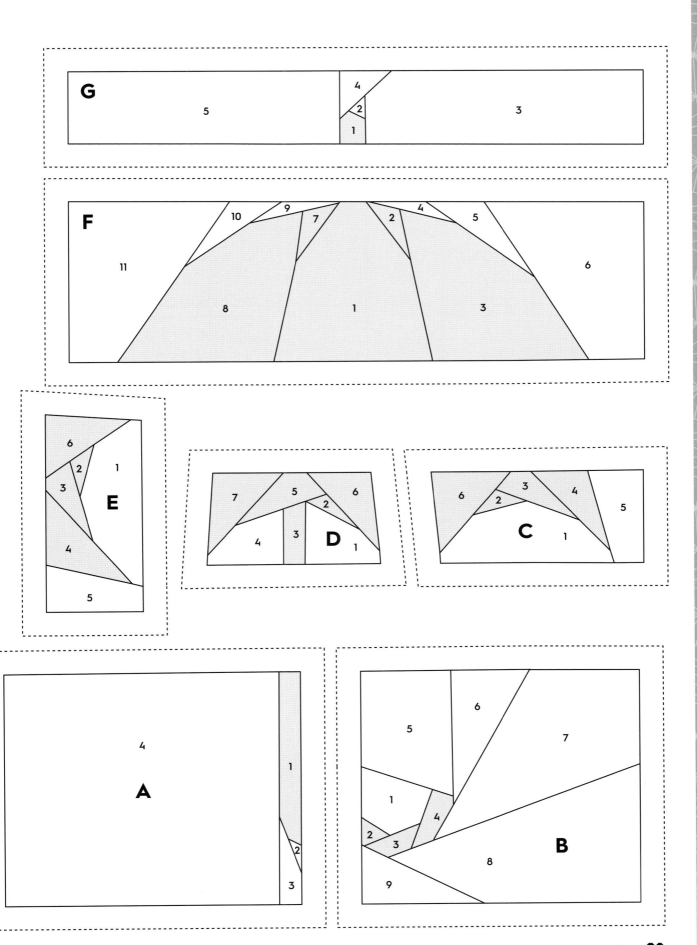

RAINBOW

Susan White

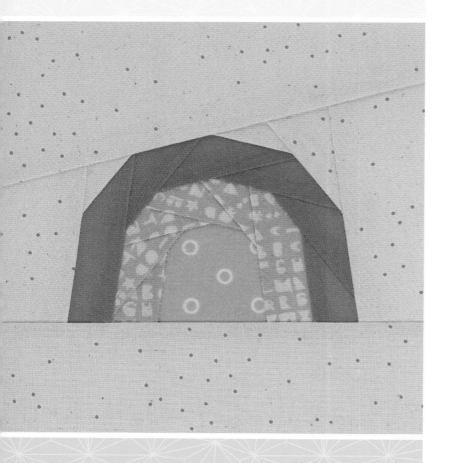

YOU WILL NEED

* One fat eighth of cream print fabric
* Smaller scraps of bright pink, lime green and turquoise fabrics

BLOCK CONSTRUCTION

Make one copy of pattern A.

Complete section A.

REFERENCE DIAGRAM

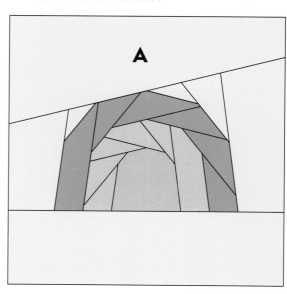

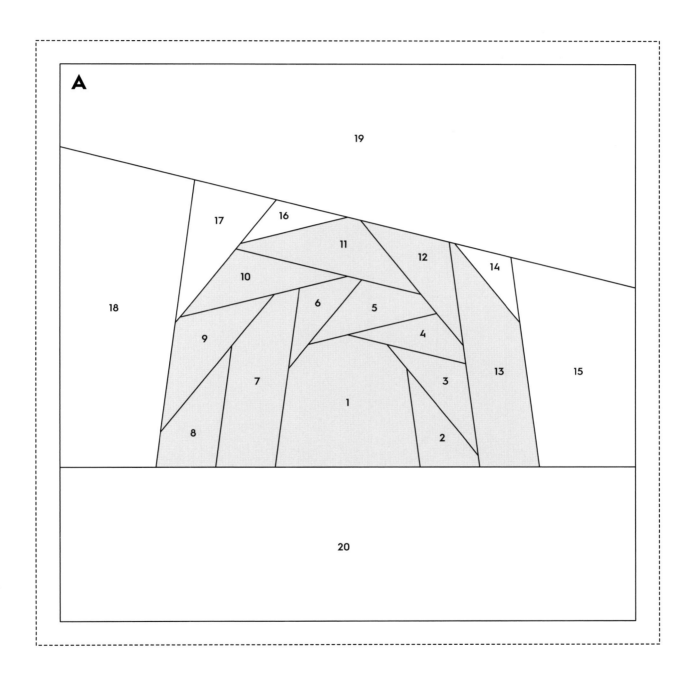

RAINDROP

Susan White

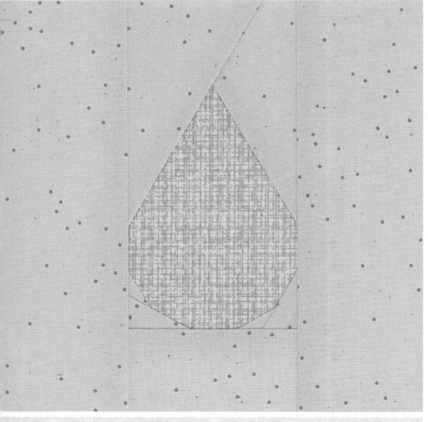

YOU WILL NEED

- One fat eighth of cream print fabric
- Smaller scrap of blue fabric

BLOCK CONSTRUCTION

Make one copy of pattern A.

Complete section A.

REFERENCE DIAGRAM

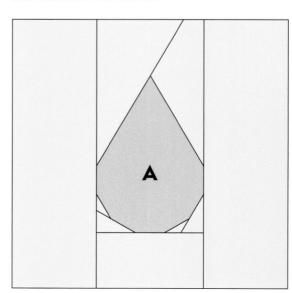

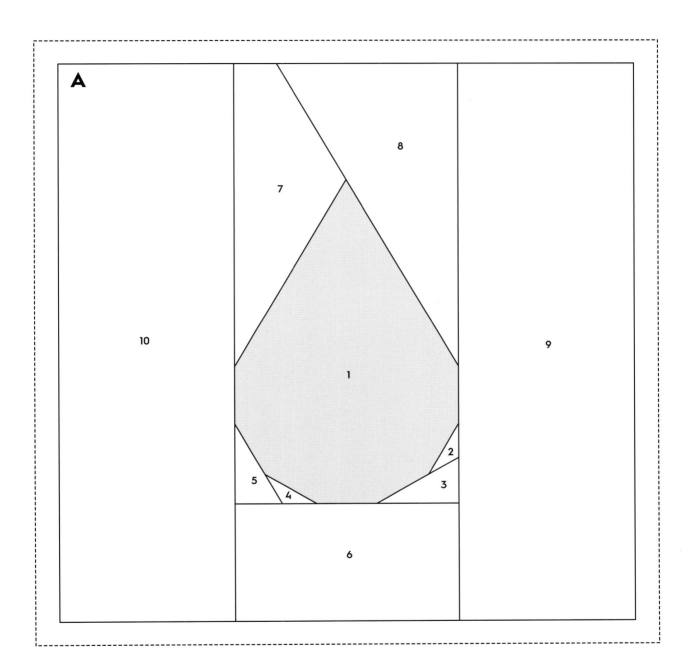

LIGHTNING

Susan White

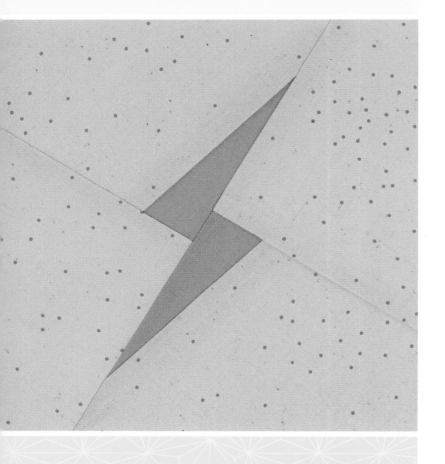

YOU WILL NEED

* One fat eighth of cream print fabric
* Smaller scrap of yellow fabric

BLOCK CONSTRUCTION

Make one copy each of patterns A and B.

Complete sections A and B.

Join A to B. Press seam towards A or B.

REFERENCE DIAGRAM

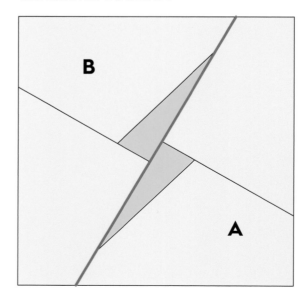

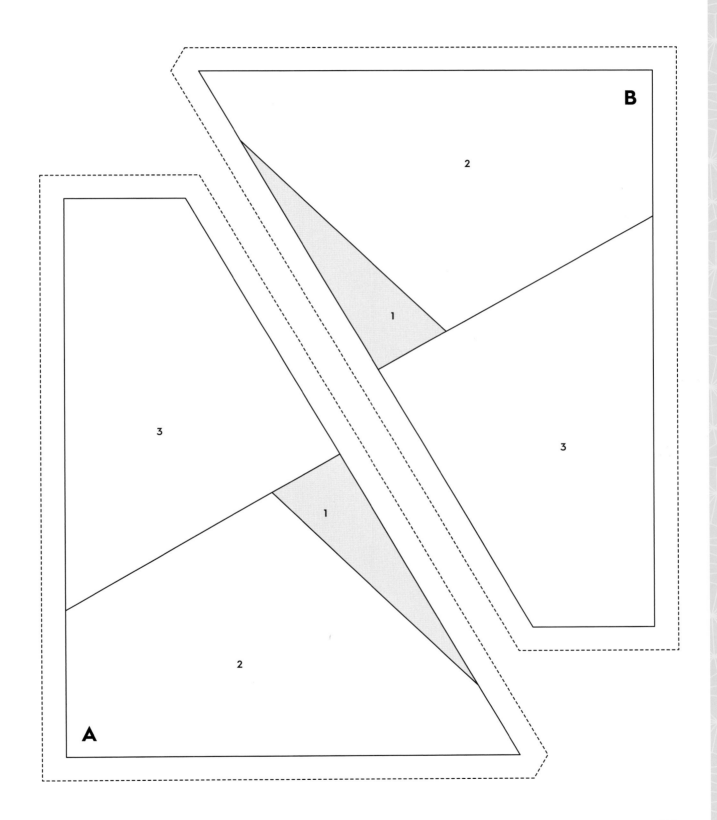

MITTENS

Kerry Green

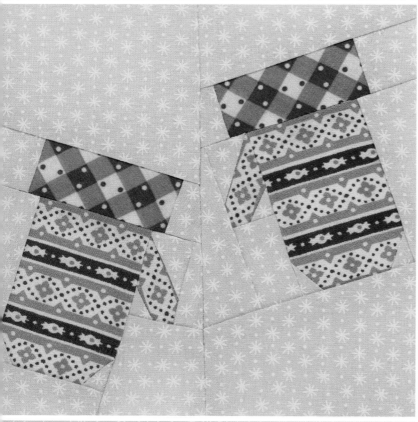

YOU WILL NEED

* Large scrap of light grey fabric, at least 16" x 16" (40.5cm x 40.5cm)
* Large scrap of lilac print fabric, at least 5" x 9" (13cm x 23cm)
* Large scrap of green print fabric, at least 2" x 8" (5cm x 20.5cm)

BLOCK CONSTRUCTION

Make one copy each of patterns A, B, C, D, E, F and G.

Complete sections A to G.

Join A to B. Press seam open.

Join AB to C. Press seam open.

Join D to E. Press seam open.

Join DE to F. Press seam open.

Join G to DEF. Press seam towards G.

Join ABC to DEFG. Press seam open.

REFERENCE DIAGRAM

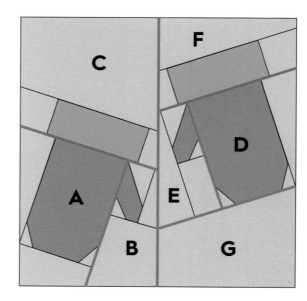

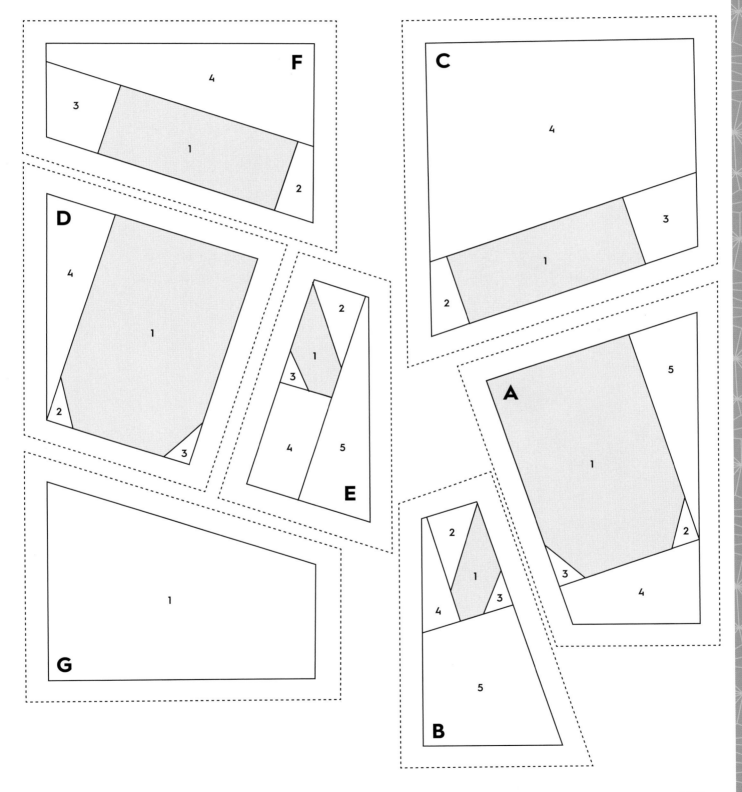

WOOLLY HAT

Kerry Green

YOU WILL NEED

* Large scrap of light grey fabric, at least 14" x 14" (35.5cm x 35.5cm)
* Smaller scraps of lilac print, mid green print and mint print fabric

BLOCK CONSTRUCTION

Make one copy each of patterns A, B and C.

Complete sections A to C.

Join A to B. Press seam open.

Join AB to C. Press seam open.

REFERENCE DIAGRAM

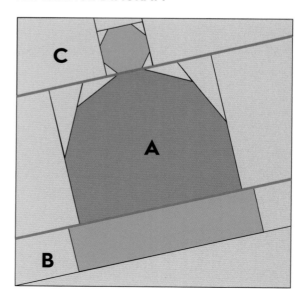

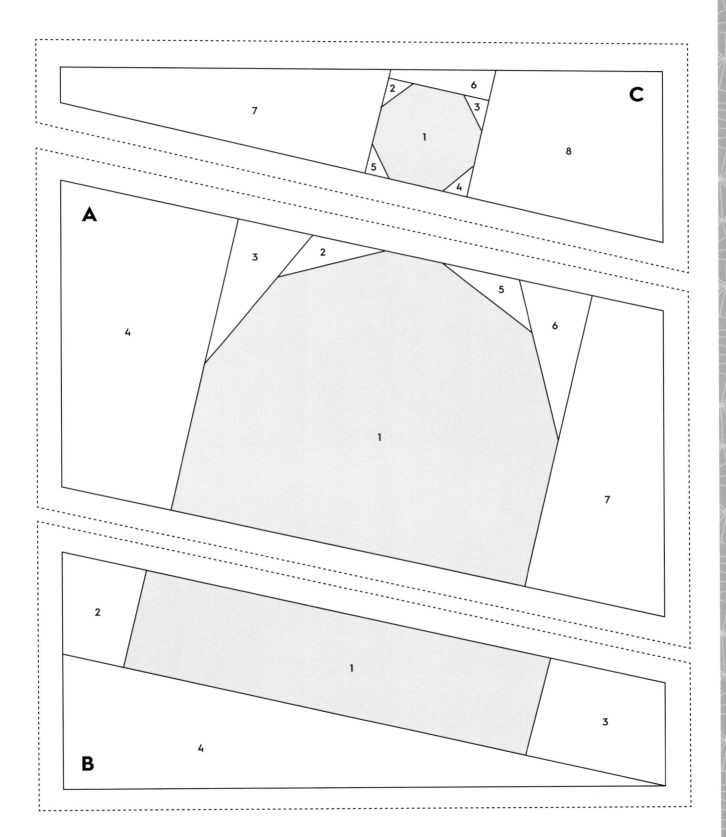

HEART

Lindsay Chieco

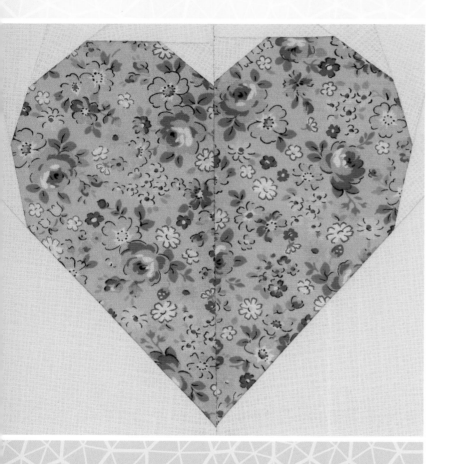

YOU WILL NEED

* Large scrap of white fabric, at least 11" x 11" (28cm x 28cm)
* Smaller scrap of aqua floral print fabric

BLOCK CONSTRUCTION

Make one copy each of patterns A and B.

Complete sections A and B.

Join A to B. Press seams open.

REFERENCE DIAGRAM

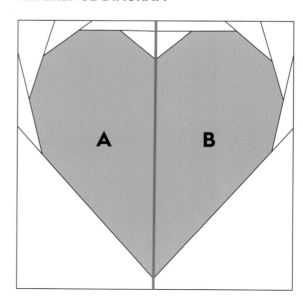

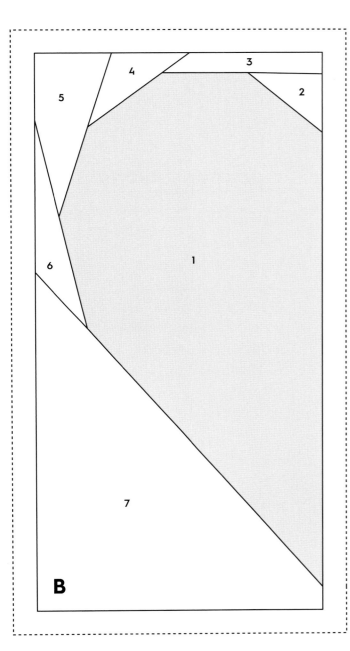

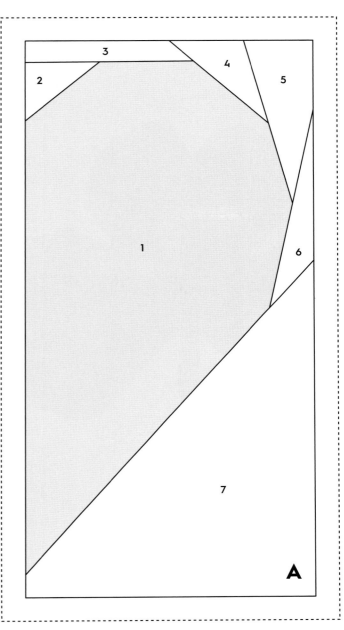

SHAMROCK

Lindsay Chieco

YOU WILL NEED

- Large scrap of white fabric, at least 11" x 11" (28cm x 28cm)
- Large scrap of green fabric, at least 7" x 7" (18cm x 18cm)

BLOCK CONSTRUCTION

Make one copy each of patterns A, B, C, D, E, F and G.

Complete sections A to G.

Join B to C. Press seams open.

Join D to E. Press seams open.

Join F to G. Press seams open.

Join FG to A. Press seam towards FG.

Join BC to DE. Press seam towards BC.

Join BCDE to FGA. Press seam towards FGA.

REFERENCE DIAGRAM

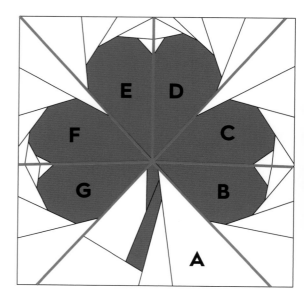

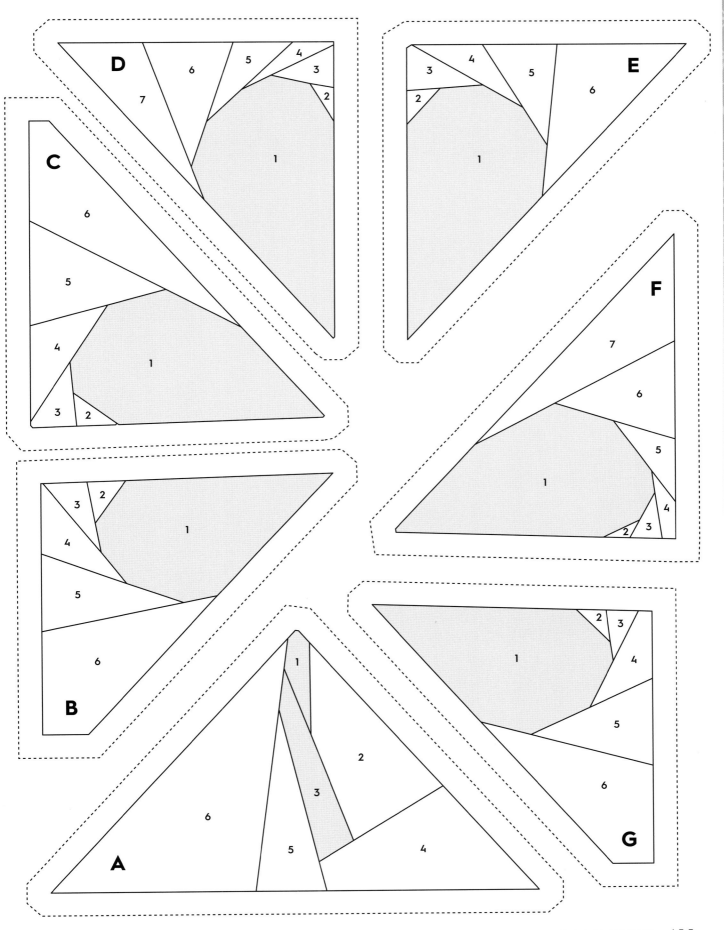

EASTER EGG

Lindsay Chieco

YOU WILL NEED

- Large scrap of white/light print fabric, at least 11" x 11" (28cm x 28cm)
- Smaller scraps of turquoise, pink, yellow and green fabrics

BLOCK CONSTRUCTION

Make one copy each of patterns A, B, C and D.

Complete sections A to D.

Join A to B. Press seam towards B.

Join AB to C. Press seam towards C.

Join ABC to D. Press seam towards D.

REFERENCE DIAGRAM

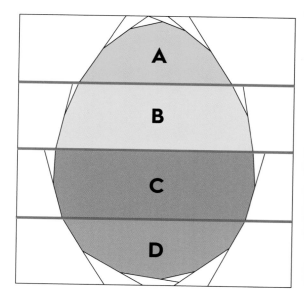

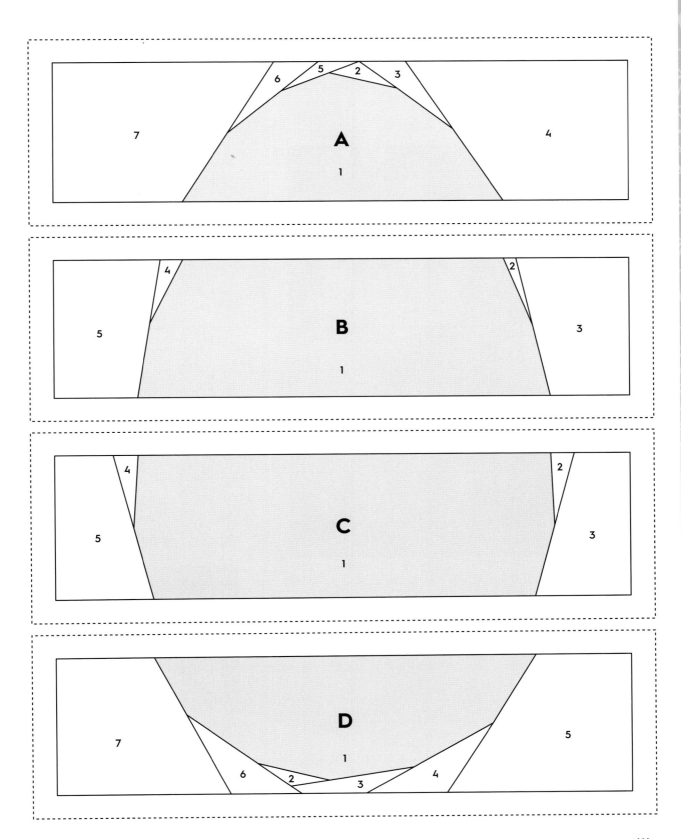

PUMPKIN
Kerry Green

YOU WILL NEED

* Large scrap of black print fabric, at least 14" x 14" (35.5cm x 35.5cm)

* Large scrap of orange fabric, at least 15" x 15" (38cm x 38cm) or smaller assorted orange scraps

* Smaller scraps of bright green and black fabrics

BLOCK CONSTRUCTION

Make one copy each of patterns A, B, C, D, E, F and G.

Complete sections A to G.

Join A to B. Press seam open.

Join C to D. Press seam open.

Join E and F to CD. Press seams towards E and F.

Join AB to CDEF. Press seam open.

Join G to ABCDEF. Press seam open.

REFERENCE DIAGRAM

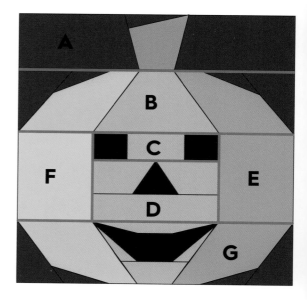

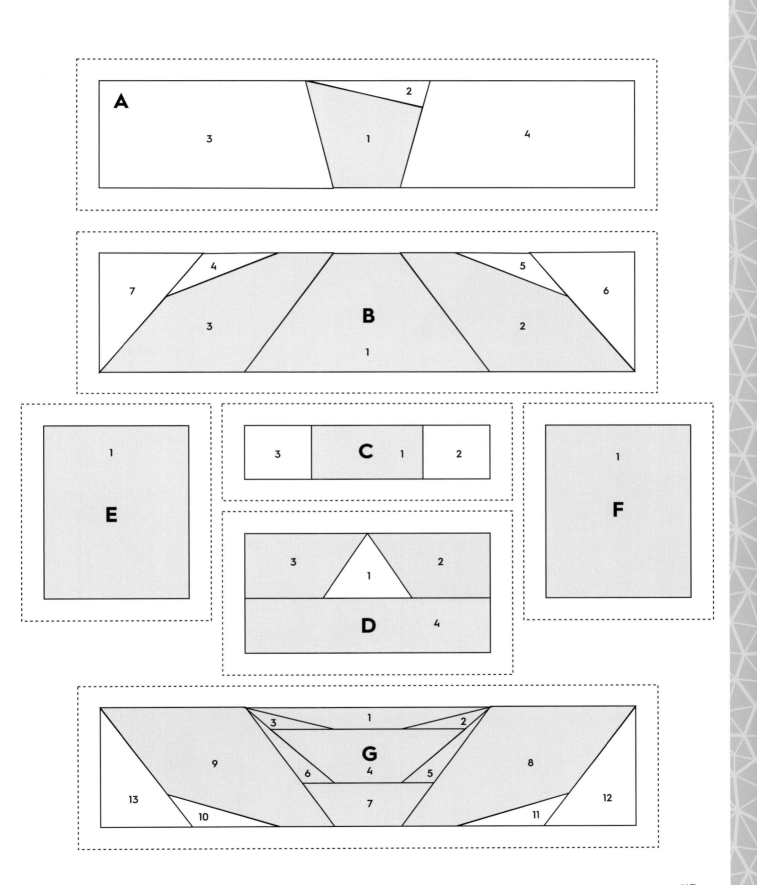

NEW HOME

Sarah Ashford

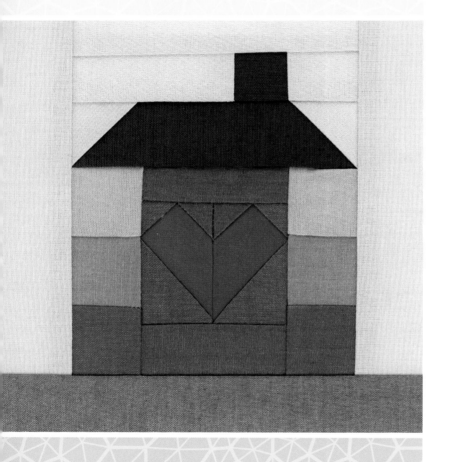

YOU WILL NEED

- Large scrap of light grey fabric, at least 6" x 6" (15.5cm x 15.5cm)
- Large scrap of green fabric, at least 7" x 1½" (18cm x 4cm)
- Smaller scraps of red and assorted blue fabrics

BLOCK CONSTRUCTION

Make one copy each of patterns A, B, C, D, E, F, G, H, I, J and K.

Complete sections A to K.

Join A to B. Press seam open.

Join C and D to AB. Press seam towards C and D.

Join E and F to ABCD. Press seams towards E and F.

Join G to H. Press seam towards G.

Join GH to ABCDEF. Press seam towards ABCDEF.

Join I, J and K to ABCDEFGH. Press seams towards I, J and K.

REFERENCE DIAGRAM

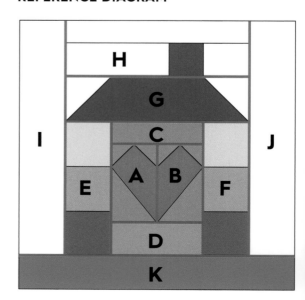

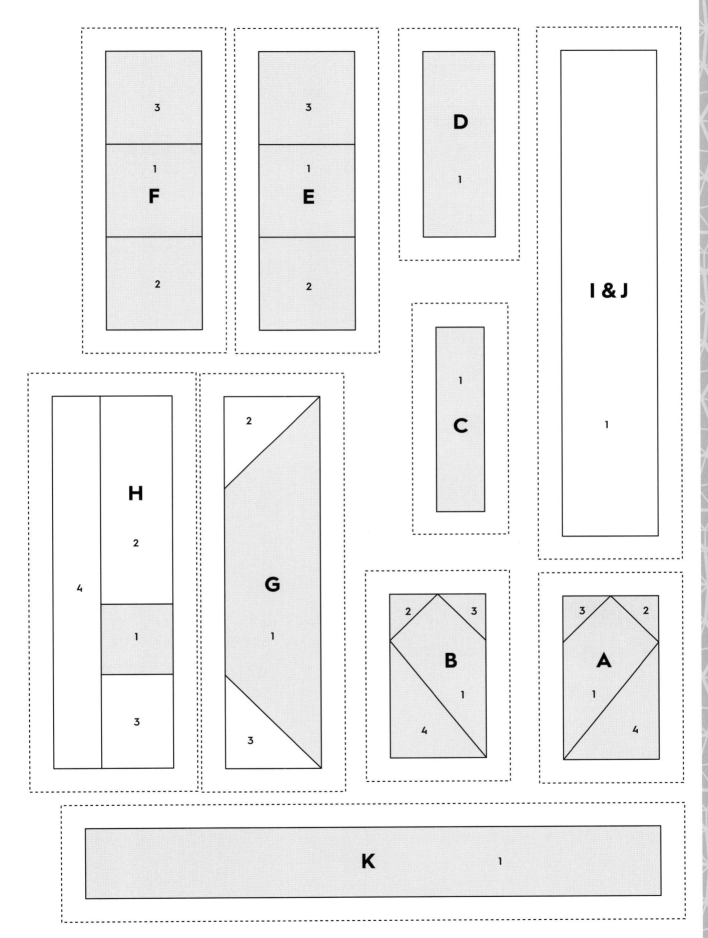

GIFT BOX

Lindsay Chieco

YOU WILL NEED

* Large scrap of blue fabric, at least 11" x 11" (28cm x 28cm)

* Large scrap of red fabric, at least for 6" x 6" (15.5cm x 15.5cm)

* Smaller scrap of stripe fabric

BLOCK CONSTRUCTION

Make one copy each of patterns A, B, C and D.

Complete sections A to D.

Join A to C. Press seam towards C.

Join AC to B. Press seam towards AC

Join ACB to D. Press seam towards D.

REFERENCE DIAGRAM

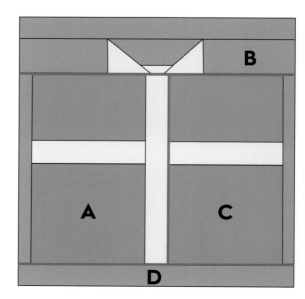

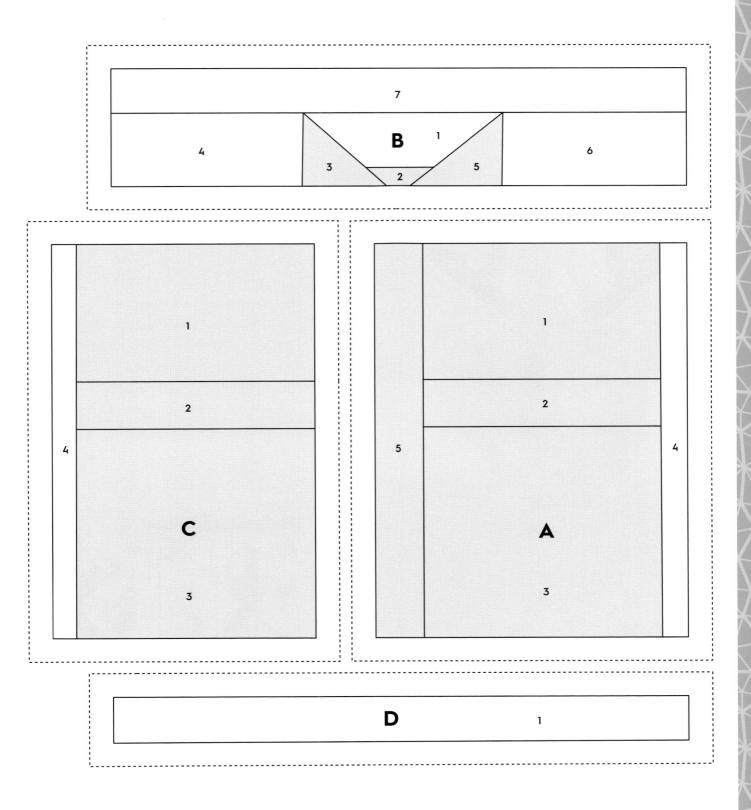

REINDEER

Kristy Lea

YOU WILL NEED

- One fat eighth of white/light print fabric
- Large scrap of black fabric, at least 6" x 9" (15.5cm x 23cm)
- Smaller scraps of assorted blue fabrics

BLOCK CONSTRUCTION

Make one copy of patterns A, B, C, D, E, F and G.

Complete sections A to G.

Join A to B. Press seam towards A.

Join C to D. Press seam towards C.

Join AB to CD. Press seam towards AB.

Join E to F. Press seam towards F.

Join G to EF. Press seam towards G.

Join ABCD to EFG. Press seam towards EFG.

REFERENCE DIAGRAM

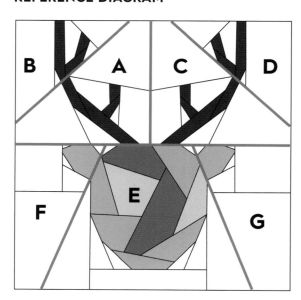

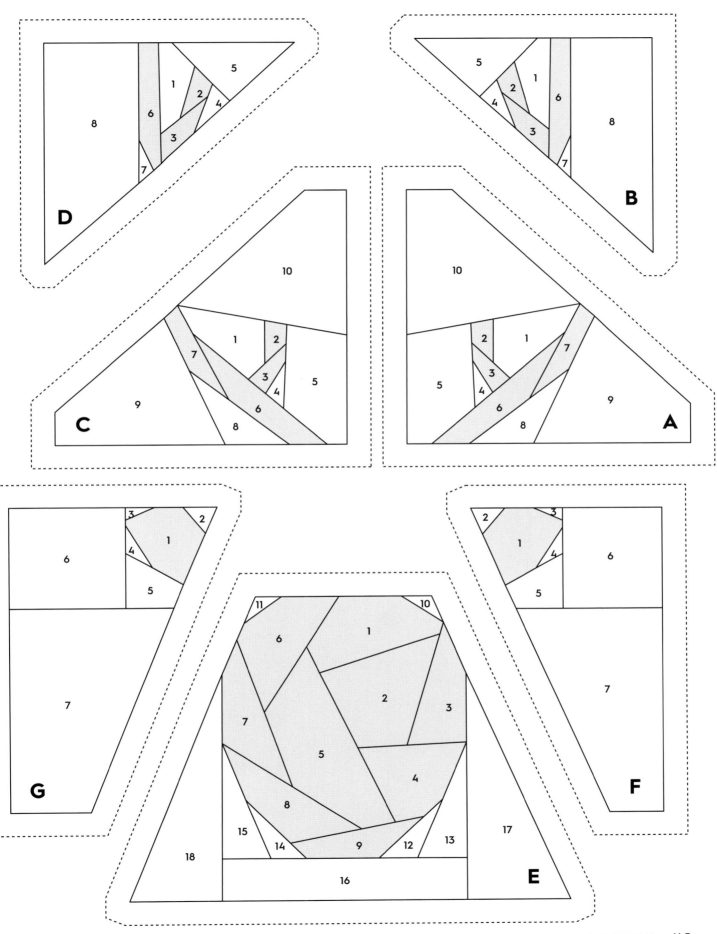

FESTIVE TREE

Lindsay Chicco

YOU WILL NEED

* Large scrap of white/light print fabric, at least 11" x 11" (28cm x 28cm)
* Smaller scraps of green, yellow and light tan fabrics

BLOCK CONSTRUCTION

Make one copy each of patterns A, B, C, D, E, F and G.

Complete sections A to G.

Join B to G. Press seam towards G.

Join BG to C. Press seam towards BG.

Join BGC to D. Press seam towards D.

Join BGCD to E. Press seam towards E.

Join BGCDE to F. Press seam towards F.

Join BGCDEF to A. Press seam towards A.

REFERENCE DIAGRAM

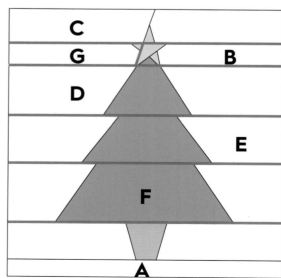

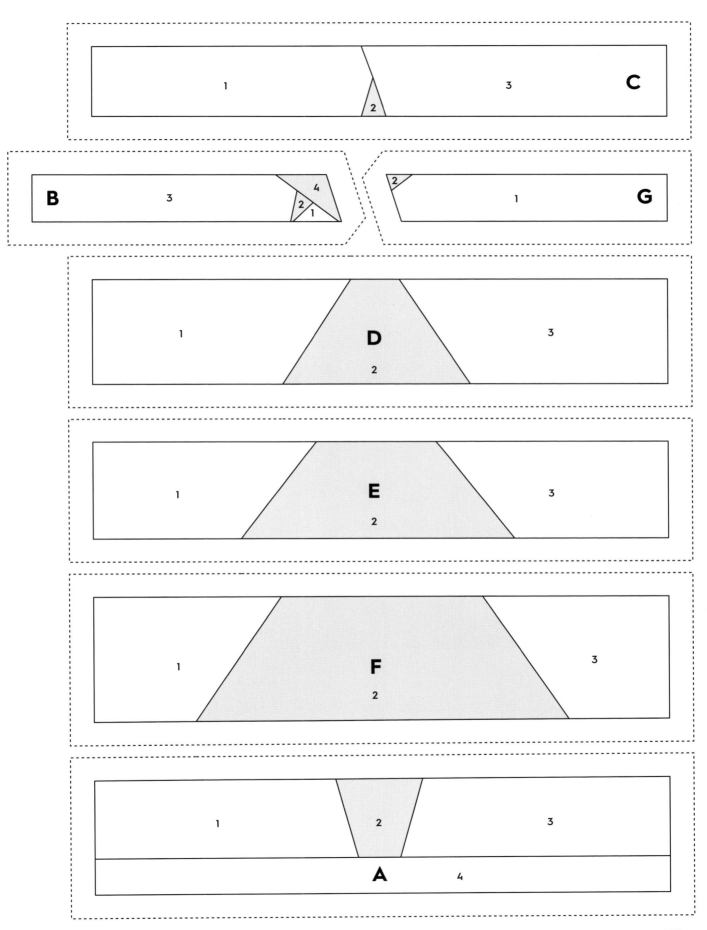

ANGEL

Joanne Hart

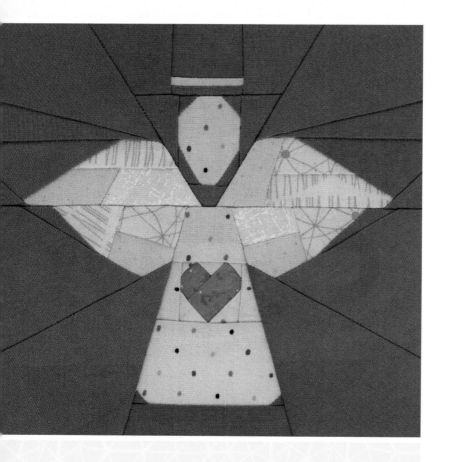

YOU WILL NEED

* One fat eighth of grey fabric
* Smaller scraps of pink, yellow, red, and assorted white and cream fabrics

BLOCK CONSTRUCTION

Make one copy each of patterns A, B, C, D, E, F and G.

Complete sections A to G.

Join A to B. Press seam towards A.

Join AB to C. Press seam towards AB.

Join ABC to D. Press seam towards ABC.

Join E to F. Press seam towards the F.

Join EF to G. Press seam towards the EF.

Join ABCD to EFG. Press seam towards EFG.

REFERENCE DIAGRAM

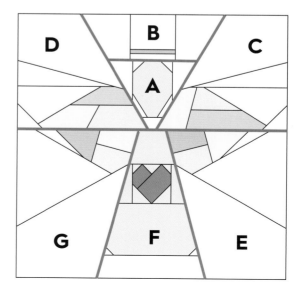

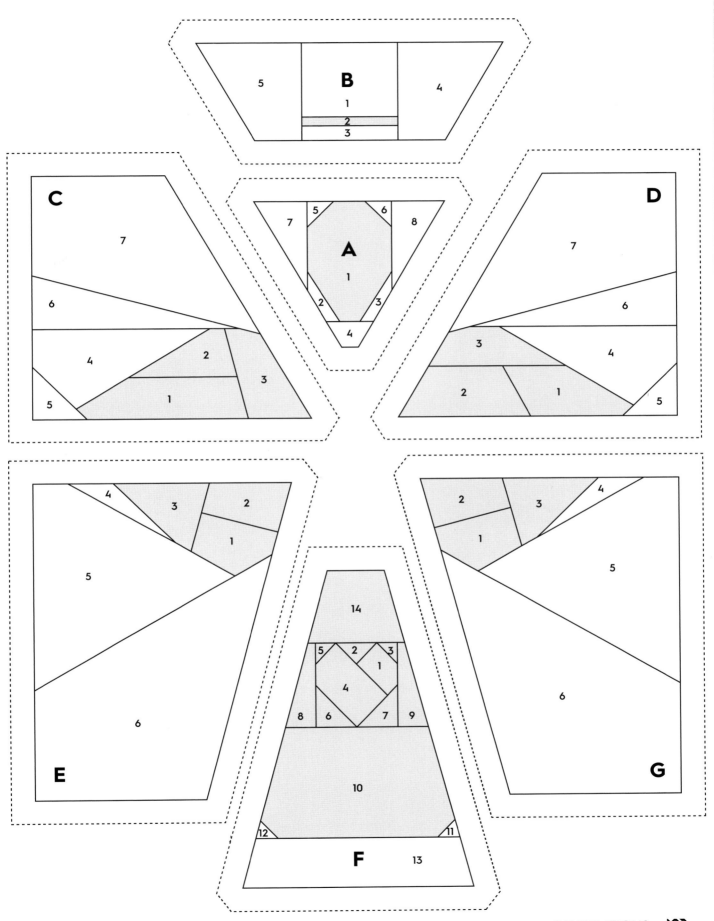

STOCKING

Lindsay Chieco

YOU WILL NEED

- Large scrap of white fabric, at least 11" x 11" (28cm x 28cm)
- Smaller scraps of light green, mid green and navy blue fabrics

BLOCK CONSTRUCTION

Make one copy each of patterns A, B, C, D and E.

Complete sections A to E.

Join A to B. Press seam towards B.

Join AB to C. Press seam towards C.

Join D to E. Press seam towards E.

Join ABC to DE. Press seam towards DE.

REFERENCE DIAGRAM

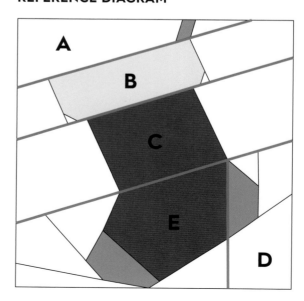

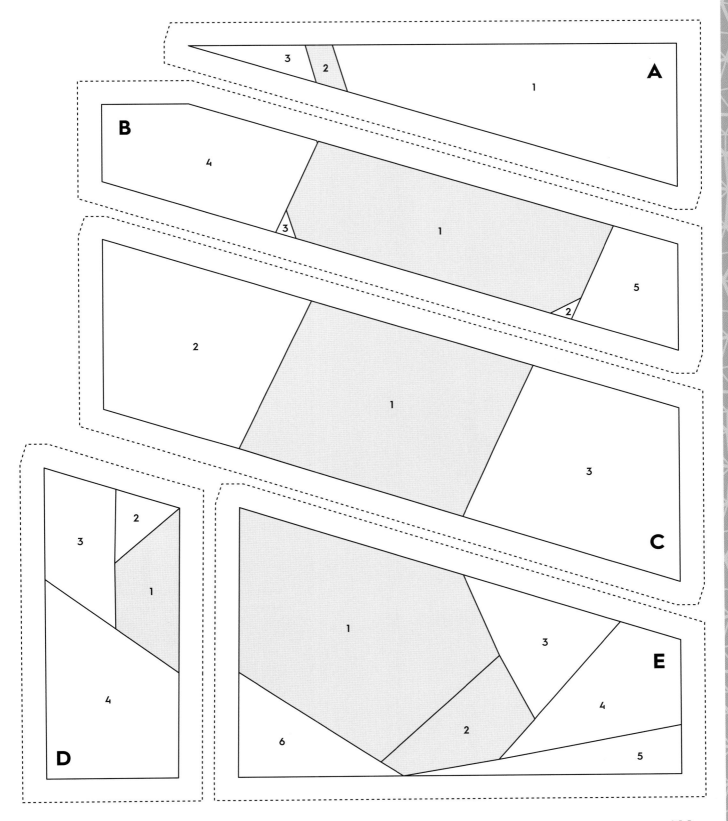

BAUBLE
Joanne Hart

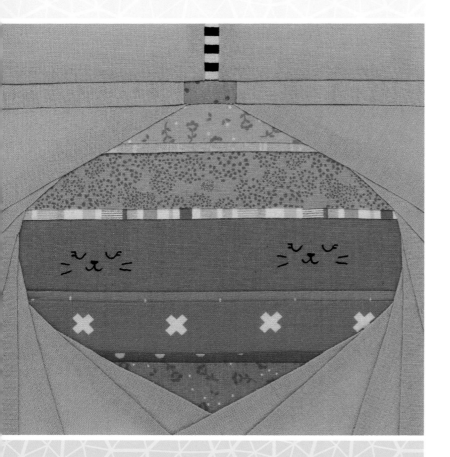

YOU WILL NEED

* One fat eighth of grey fabric
* Smaller scraps of black and white stripe and assorted pink, red, orange and yellow fabrics

BLOCK CONSTRUCTION

Make one copy each of patterns A, B and C.

Complete sections A to C.

Join A to B. Press seam towards B.

Join AB to C. Press seam towards C.

REFERENCE DIAGRAM

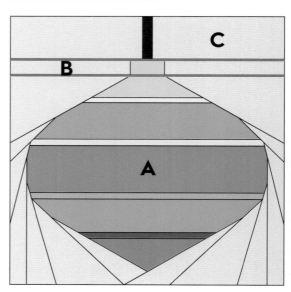

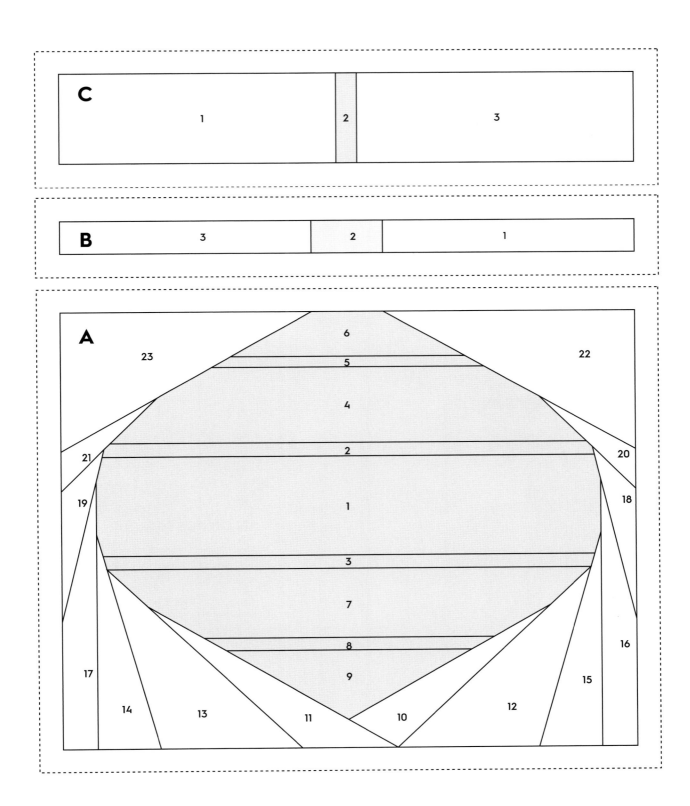

SUGAR BOWL
Kerry Green

YOU WILL NEED

- Large scrap of yellow fabric, at least 15" x 15" (38cm x 38cm)
- Large scrap of light print fabric, at least 7" x 7" (18cm x 18cm)
- Smaller scraps of mint green and light grey fabrics

BLOCK CONSTRUCTION

Make one copy each of patterns A, B, C and D.

Complete sections A to D.

Join A to B. Press seam open.

Join AB to C. Press seam open.

Join ABC to D. Press seam open.

REFERENCE DIAGRAM

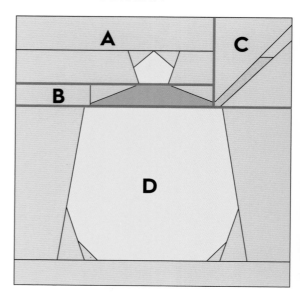

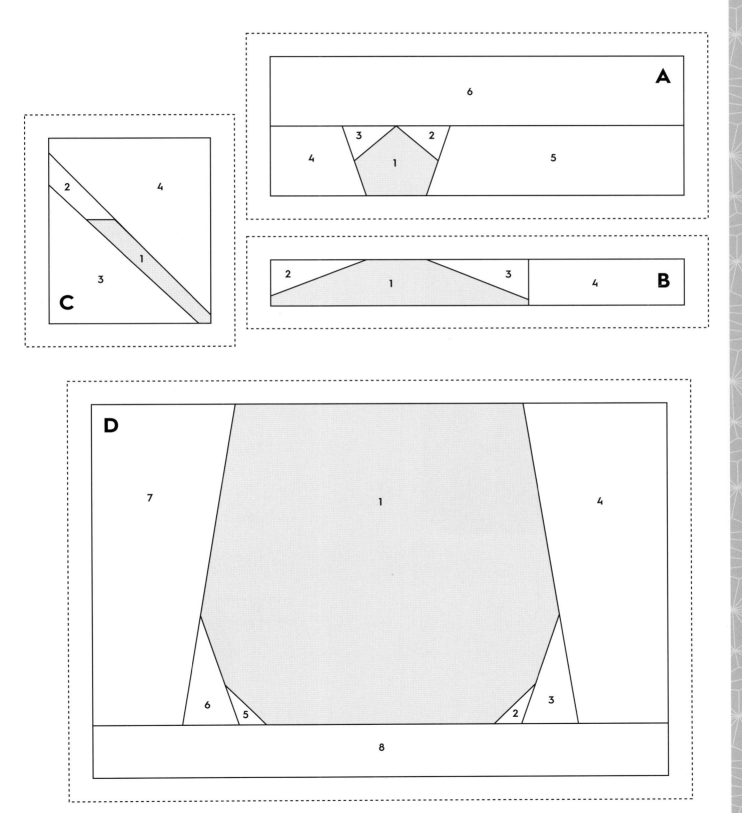

JAM JAR

Lindsay Chieco

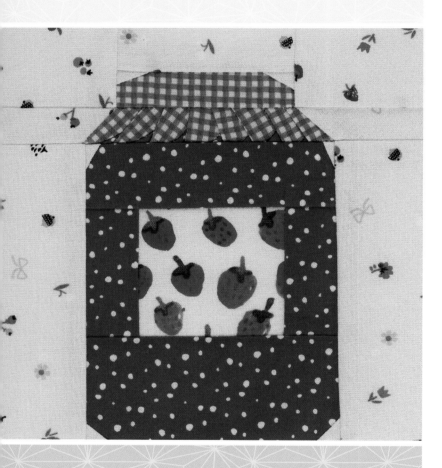

YOU WILL NEED

* Large scrap of white/light print fabric, at least 11" x 11" (28cm x 28cm)
* Smaller scraps of green gingham and red fabrics, including fussy cut strawberry print for the label

BLOCK CONSTRUCTION

Make one copy each of patterns A, B and C.

Complete sections A to C.

Join C to B. Press seam towards B.

Join CB to A. Press seam towards A.

REFERENCE DIAGRAM

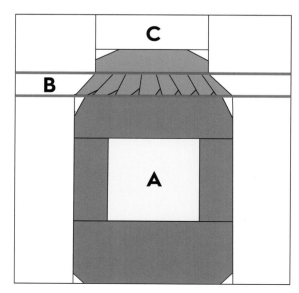

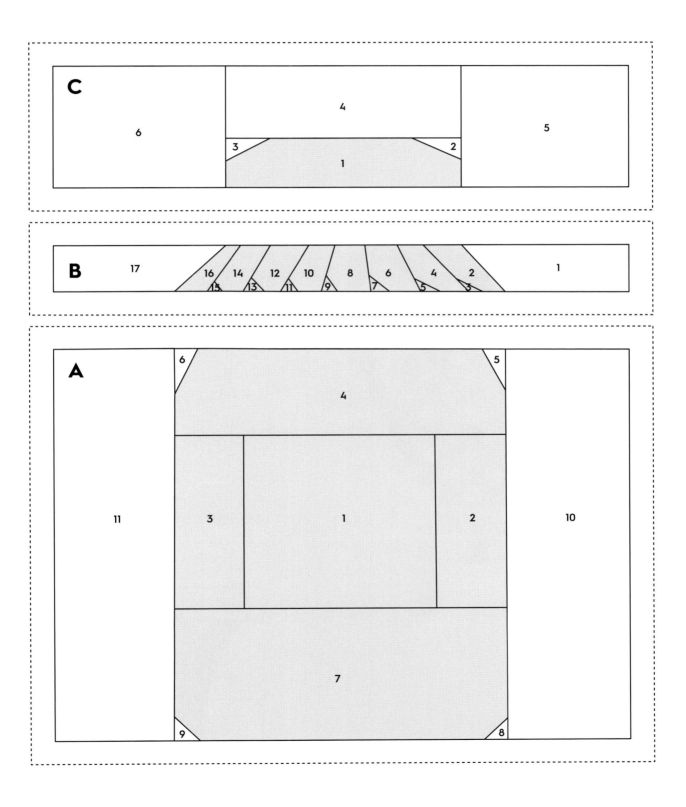

TEAPOT

Monika Henry

YOU WILL NEED

* Large scrap of white fabric, at least 8" x 12" (20.5cm x 30.5cm)

* Large scrap of red polka dot fabric, at least 4" x 8" (10cm x 20.5cm)

* Large scrap of blue fabric, at least 3½" x 7" (9cm x 18cm)

BLOCK CONSTRUCTION

Make one copy each of patterns A, B, C, D, E and F.

Complete sections A to F.

Join E to D. Press seam towards D.

Join ED to C. Press seam towards ED.

Join A to B. Press seam towards A.

Join AB to CDE. Press seam towards AB.

Join F to ABCDE. Press seam towards F.

REFERENCE DIAGRAM

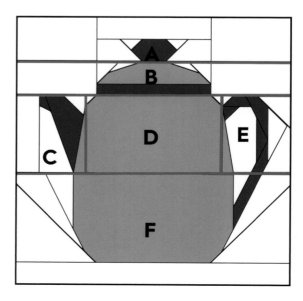

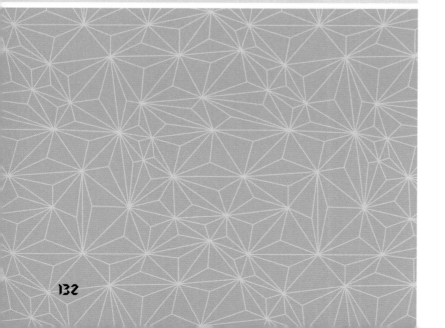

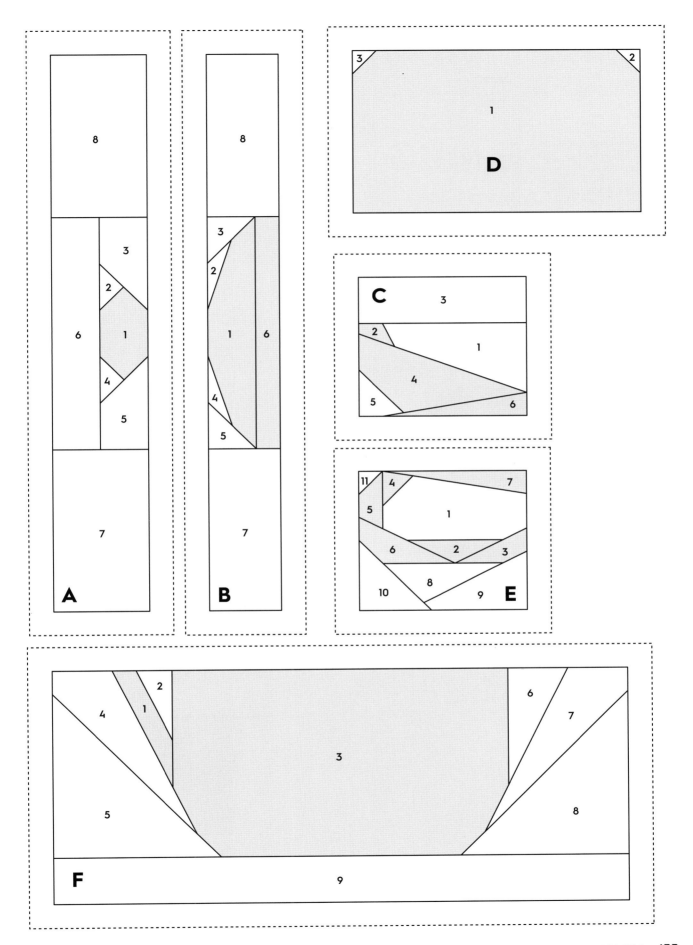

COFFEE MUG

Kerry Green

YOU WILL NEED

- Large scrap of white/light print fabric, at least 14" x 14" (35.5cm x 35.5cm)
- Large scrap of turquoise fabric, at least 10" x 10" (25.5cm x 25.5cm)

BLOCK CONSTRUCTION

Make one copy each of patterns A, B, C and D.

Complete sections A to D.

Join A to B. Press seam open.

Join C to AB. Press seam towards C.

Join D to ABC. Press seam towards D.

REFERENCE DIAGRAM

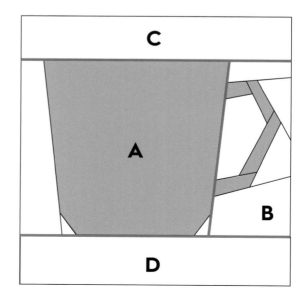

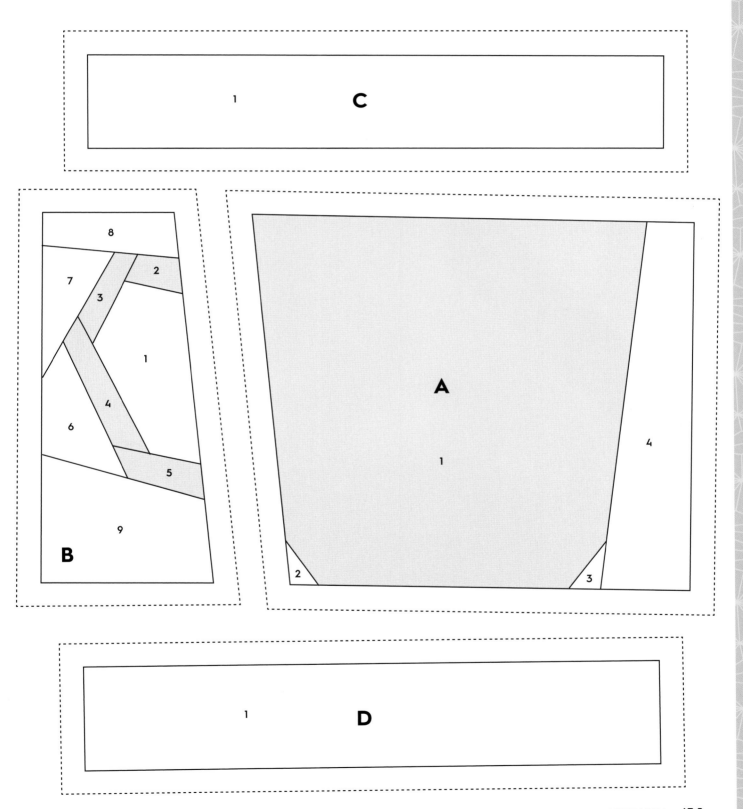

ROLLING PIN

Susan White

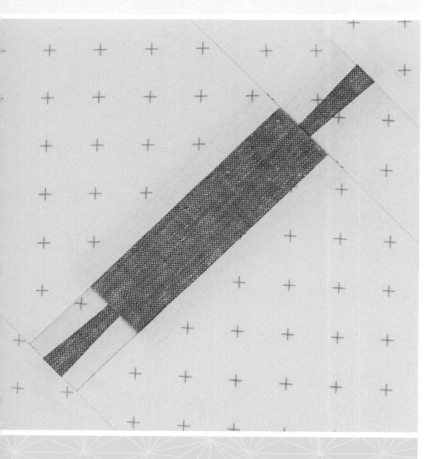

YOU WILL NEED

- One fat eighth of white/light print fabric
- Smaller scrap of brown fabric

BLOCK CONSTRUCTION

Make one copy each of patterns A and B.

Complete sections A and B.

Join A to B. Press seam towards A.

REFERENCE DIAGRAM

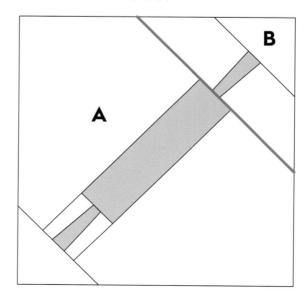

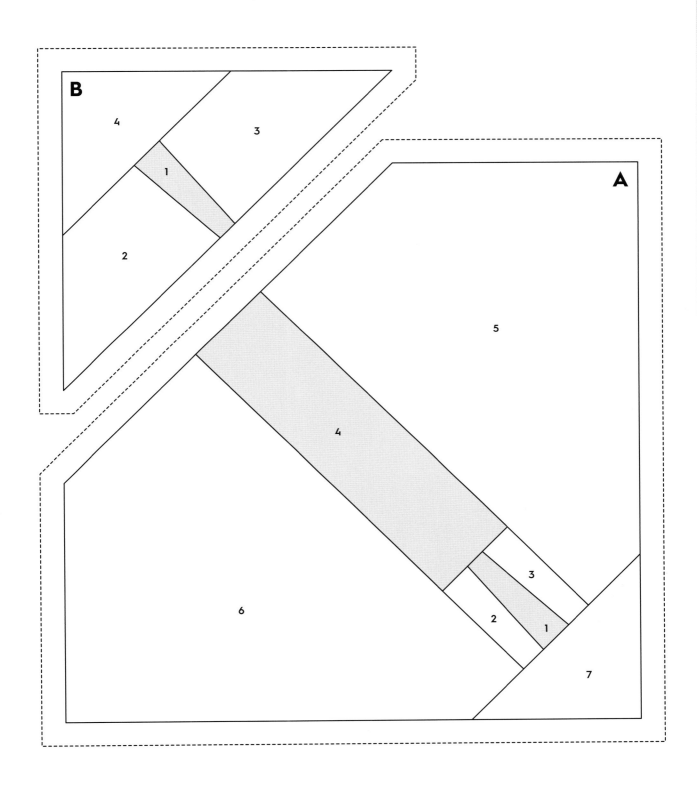

EGG CUP

Monika Henry

YOU WILL NEED

* Large scrap of light blue fabric, at least 7" x 18" (18cm x 45.5cm)
* Smaller scraps of red polka dot and white fabrics

BLOCK CONSTRUCTION

Make one copy each of patterns A, B, C and D.

Complete sections A to D.

Join A to B. Press seam towards B.

Join C to D. Press seam towards C.

Join AB to CD. Press seam towards CD.

REFERENCE DIAGRAM

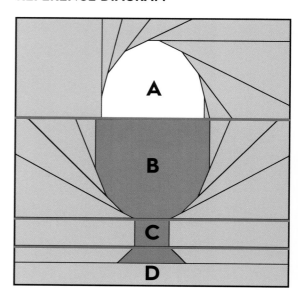

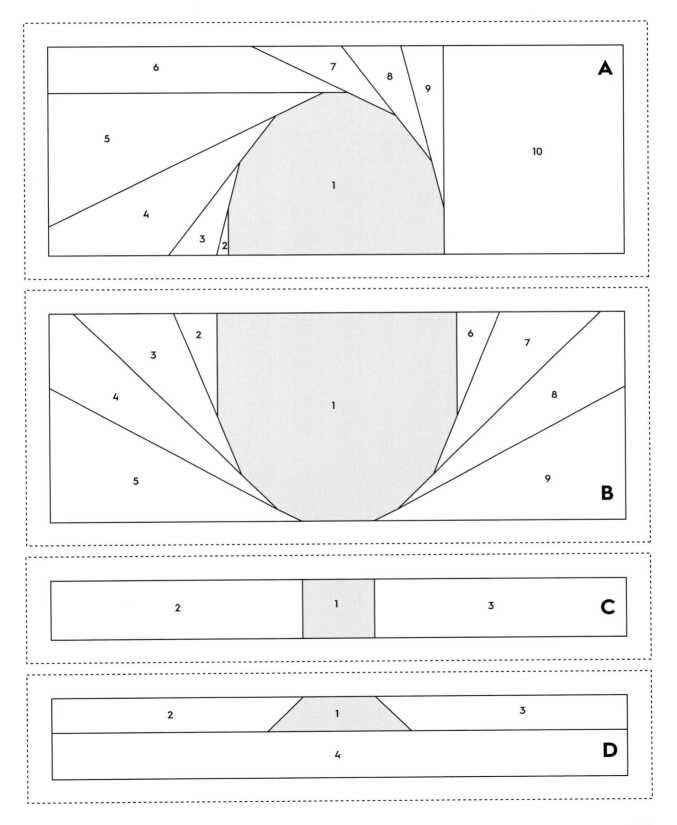

MEASURING JUG

Susan White

YOU WILL NEED

* One fat eighth of pink fabric
* Smaller scraps of white and white print fabrics

BLOCK CONSTRUCTION

Make one copy each of patterns A and B.

Complete sections A and B.

Join A to B. Press seam towards B.

REFERENCE DIAGRAM

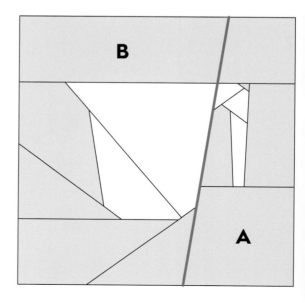

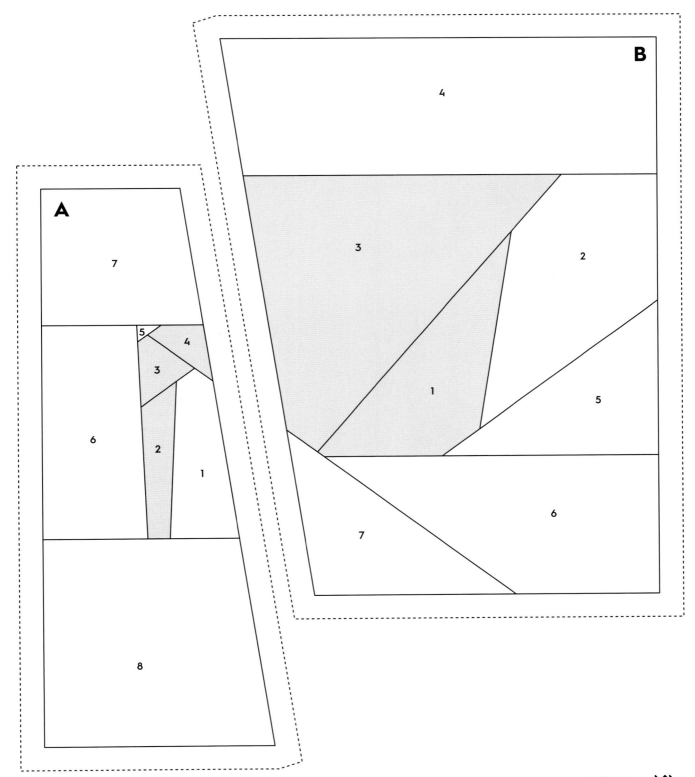

KITCHEN SCALES

Charise Randell

YOU WILL NEED

- One fat eighth of white fabric
- Large scrap of blue fabric, at least 10" x 10" (25.5cm x 25.5cm)
- Smaller scraps of red fabrics
- Red and gold embroidery threads

BLOCK CONSTRUCTION

Make one copy each of patterns A, B, C, D, E, F and G.

Complete sections A to G.

Join A to B. Press seam towards A.

Join C to D. Press seam towards C.

Join AB to CD. Press seam open.

Join E to F. Press seam open.

Join ABCD to EF. Press seam towards EF.

Join G to ABCDEF. Press seam towards G.

Using the dial pattern and following Making a Circle Appliqué (see General Techniques), make a white circle appliqué. Sew in place (see dashed lines on reference diagram). Use red embroidery thread and satin stitch to embroider the pointer, then overstitch with widely spaced diagonal stitches using gold embroidery thread.

REFERENCE DIAGRAM

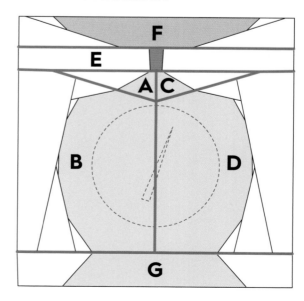

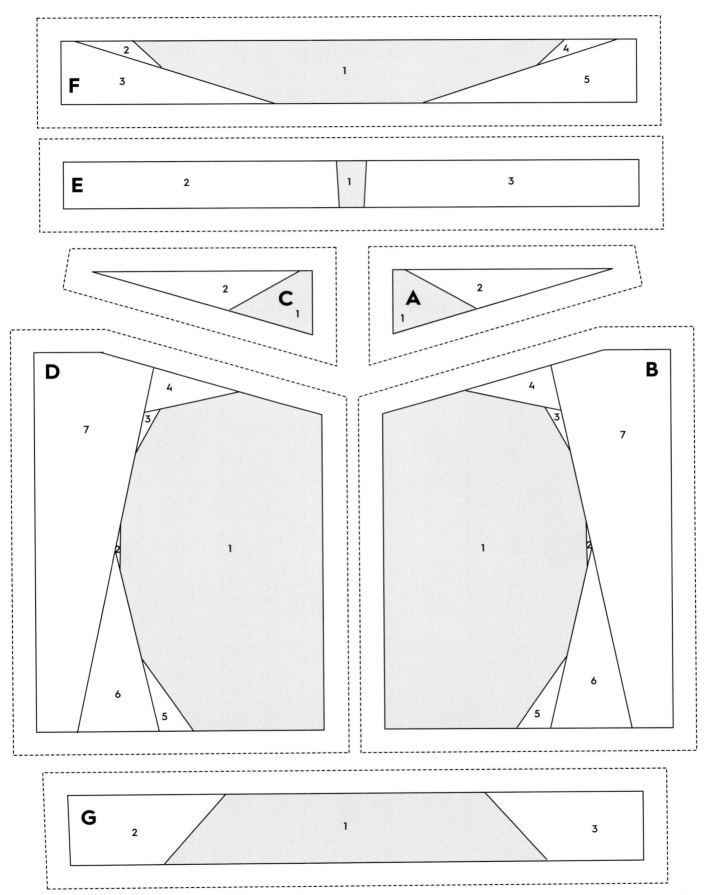

MILK CARTON

Susan White

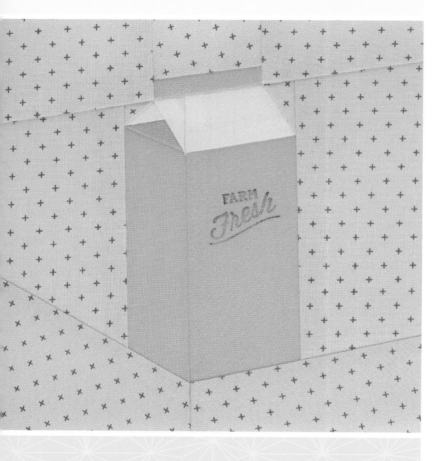

YOU WILL NEED

- One fat eighth of peach fabric
- Smaller scraps of yellow, white and grey fabrics
- Rubber stamp and fabric ink pad

BLOCK CONSTRUCTION

Make one copy each of patterns A, B and C.

Complete sections A to C.

Join A to B. Press seam towards A.

Join AB to C. Press seam towards C.

The 'Farm Fresh' branding was stamped using a rubber stamp and an ink pad designed for fabric.

REFERENCE DIAGRAM

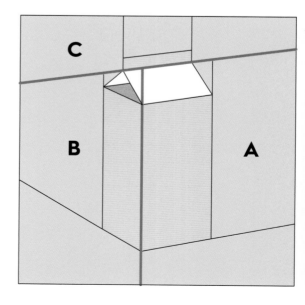

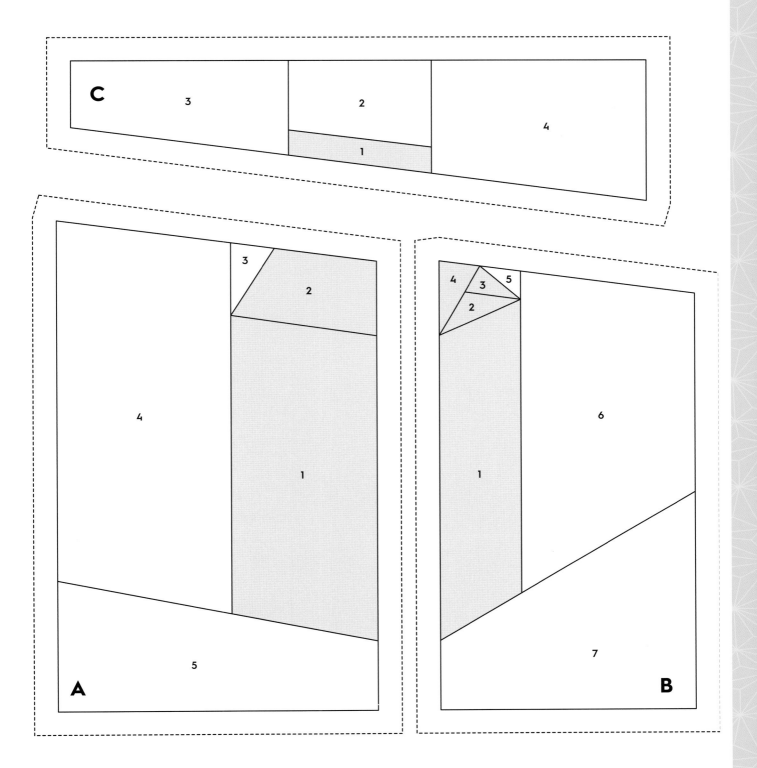

TEABAG

Monika Henry

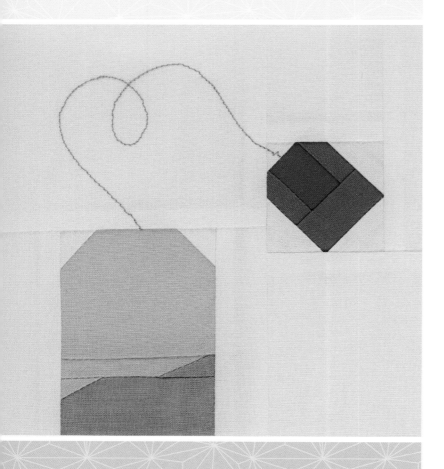

YOU WILL NEED

- Large scrap of white fabric, at least 4¼" x 15" (11cm x 38cm)
- Smaller scraps of beige, light brown, purple and blue fabrics
- Coordinating thread for teabag string

BLOCK CONSTRUCTION

Make one copy each of patterns A, B, C, D, E and F.

Complete sections A to F.

Join C to B. Press seam towards C.

Join E to BC. Press seam towards E.

Join F to BCE. Press seam towards F.

Join D to BCEF. Press seam towards D.

Join A to BCEFD. Press seam towards A.

Referring to the dashed line on the reference diagram, use a heat-erasable pen to draw the string joining teabag to tag. Using coordinating thread and regular stitch, machine stitch over the marked line; press to remove the ink.

REFERENCE DIAGRAM

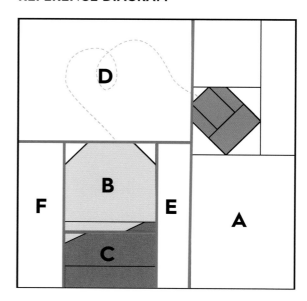

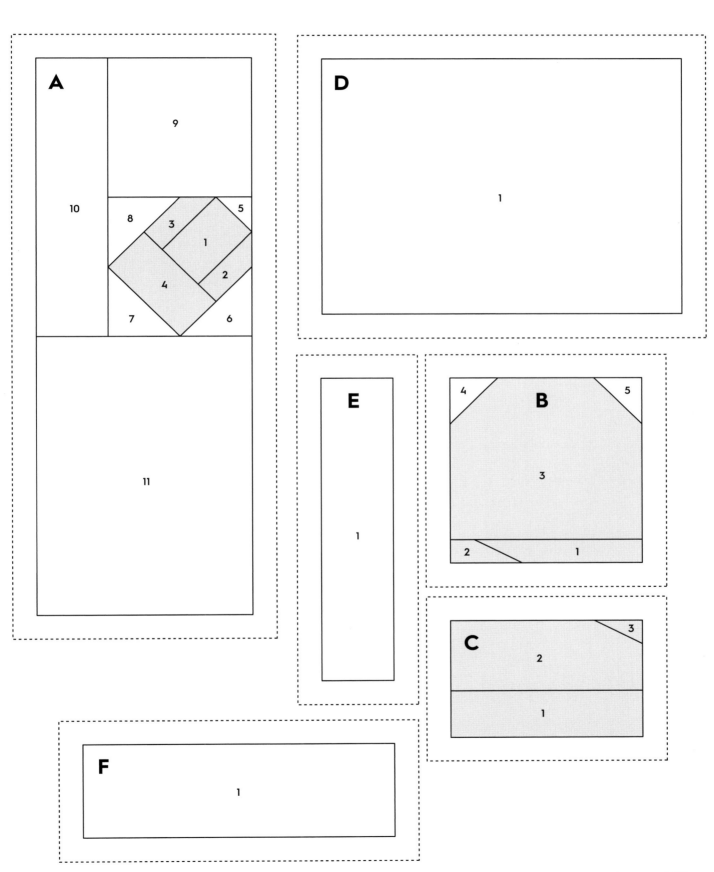

SPATULA

Susan White

YOU WILL NEED

- One fat eighth of pink fabric
- Smaller scraps of bright cherry red and white fabrics

BLOCK CONSTRUCTION

Make one copy of pattern A.

Complete section A.

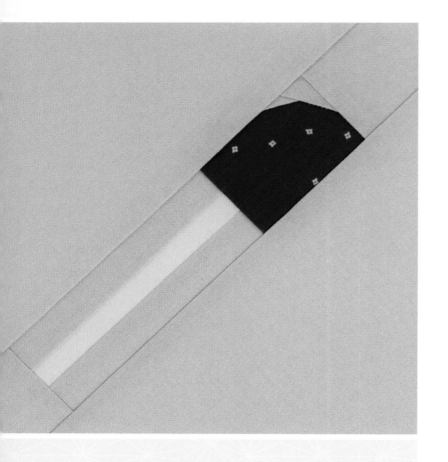

REFERENCE DIAGRAM

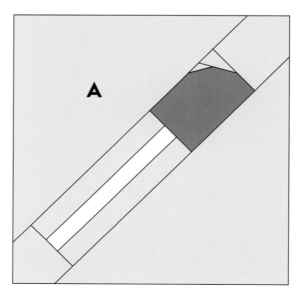

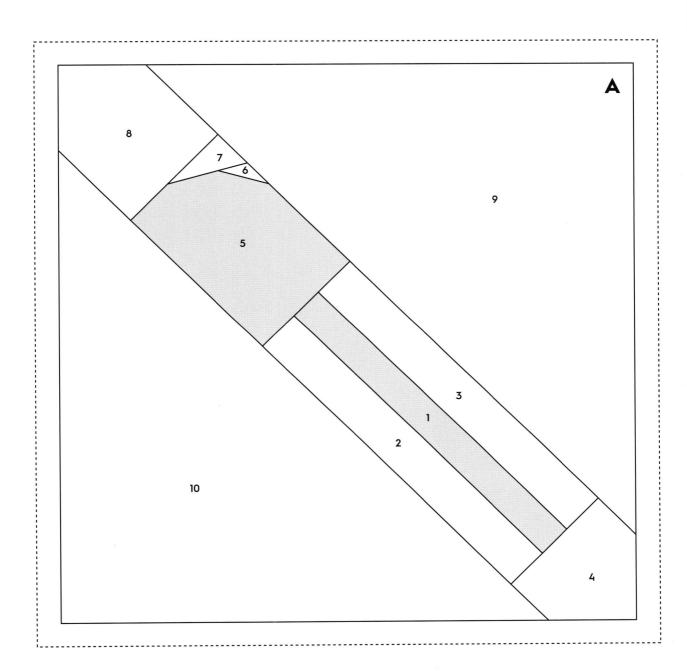

OVEN MITT

Susan White

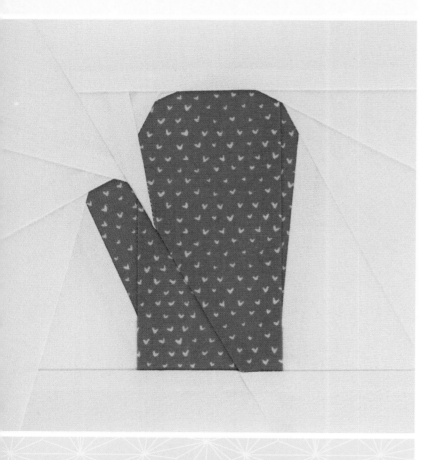

YOU WILL NEED

- One fat eighth of white fabric
- Smaller scrap of light teal fabric

BLOCK CONSTRUCTION

Make one copy each of patterns A and B.

Complete sections A and B.

Join A to B. Press seam towards A.

REFERENCE DIAGRAM

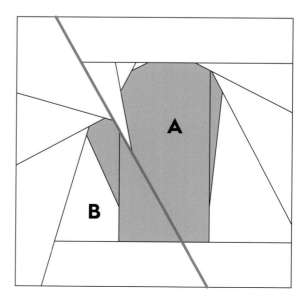

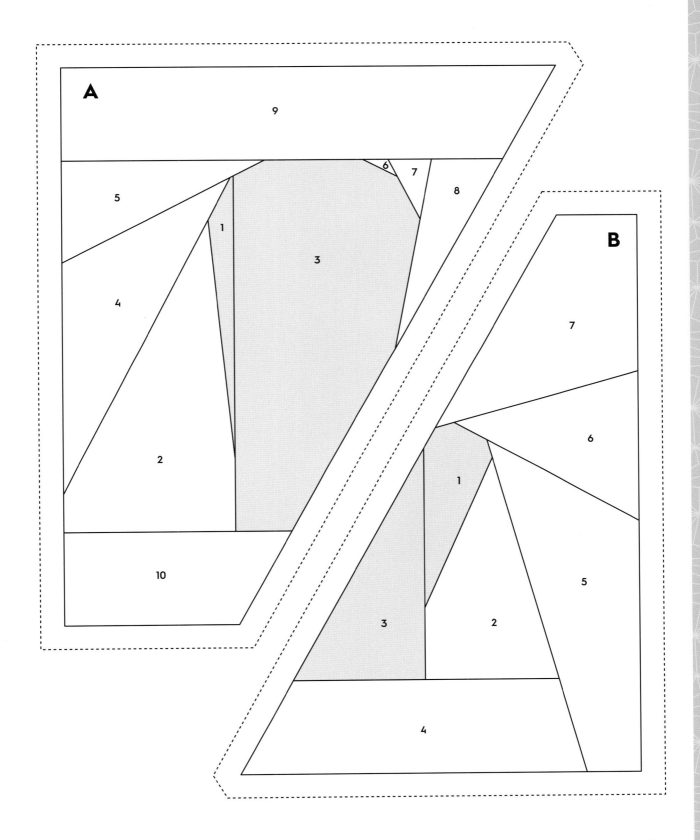

COFFEE POT

Kerry Green

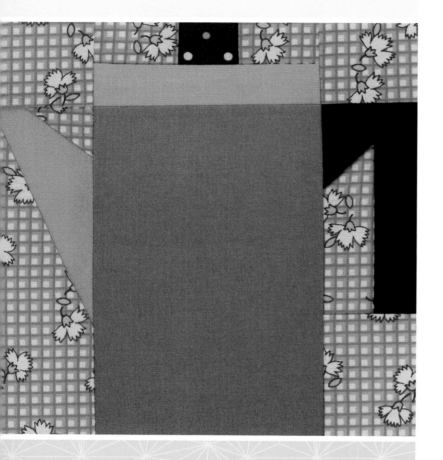

YOU WILL NEED

* Large scrap of blue fabric, at least 12" x 12" (30.5cm x 30.5cm)

* Large scrap of ombre orange fabric, at least 10" x 10" (25.5cm x 25.5cm)

* Smaller scraps of mustard yellow, brown and dark grey fabrics

BLOCK CONSTRUCTION

Make one copy each of patterns A, B and C.

Complete sections A to C.

Join A to B. Press seam open.

Join AB to C. Press seam open.

REFERENCE DIAGRAM

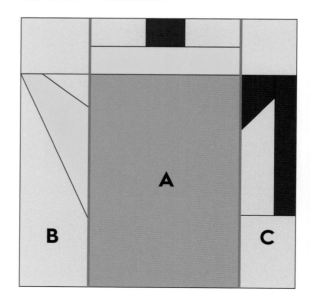

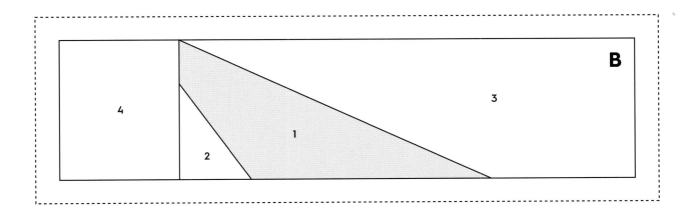

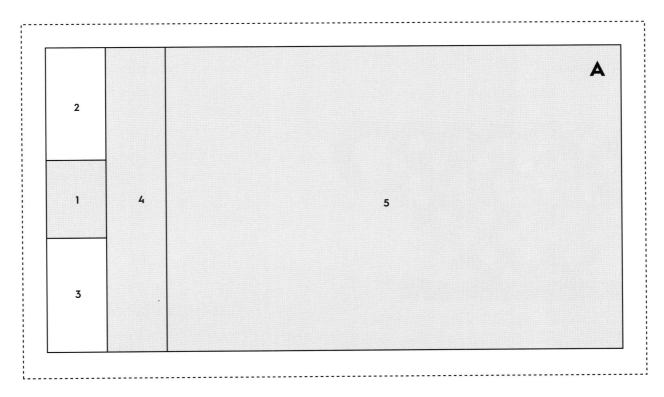

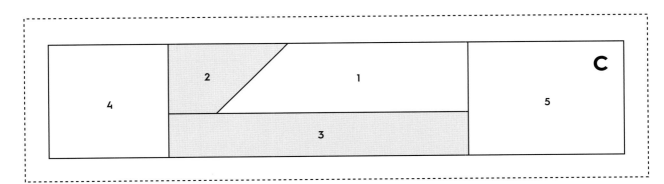

TEACUP

Monika Henry

YOU WILL NEED

* Large scrap of white fabric, at least 7" x 14" (18cm x 35.5cm)
* Smaller scraps of red polka dot, blue and grey fabrics

BLOCK CONSTRUCTION

Make one copy each of patterns A, B, C, D, E, F and G.

Complete sections A to G.

Join A to B. Press seam towards A.

Join AB to C. Press seam towards C.

Join D to E. Press seam towards E.

Join DE to F. Press seam towards F.

Join G to DEF. Press seam towards G.

Join DEFG to ABC. Press seam towards ABC.

REFERENCE DIAGRAM

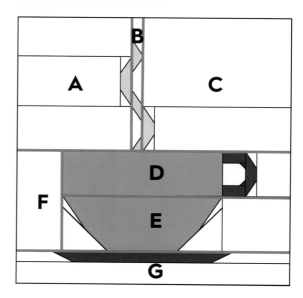

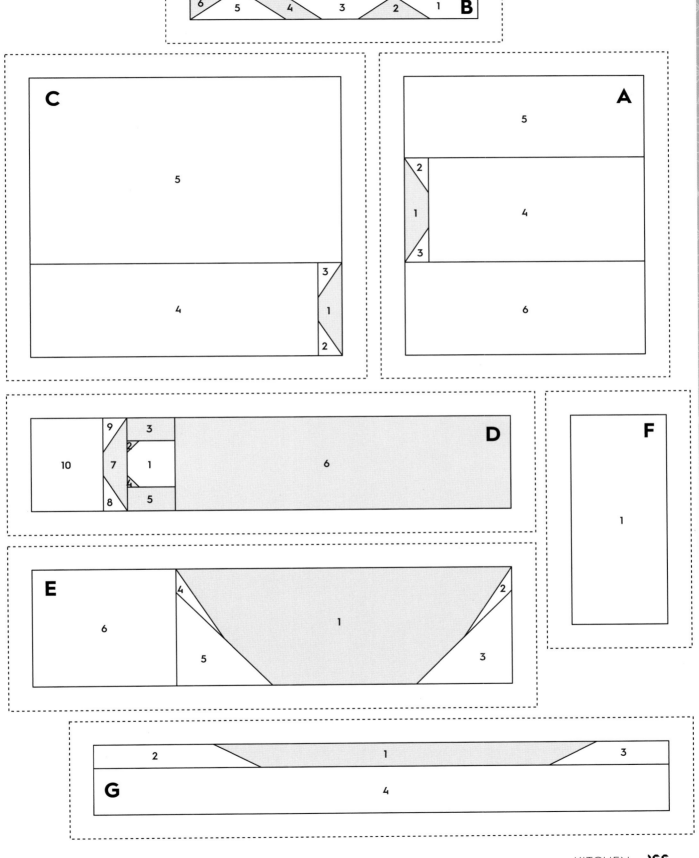

COTTAGE

Charise Randell

YOU WILL NEED

- Large scrap of yellow fabric, at least 10" x 10" (25.5cm x 25.5cm)
- Smaller scraps of turquoise gingham, light pink, mid pink, dark pink, grey and turquoise fabrics, including fussy cut prints for the windows

BLOCK CONSTRUCTION

Make one copy each of patterns A, B, C, D, E and F.

Complete sections A to F.

Join A to B. Press seam towards B.

Join C to AB. Press seam towards AB.

Join D to ABC. Press seam towards D.

Join E to ABCD. Press seam towards ABCD.

Join F to ABCDE. Press seam towards ABCDE.

REFERENCE DIAGRAM

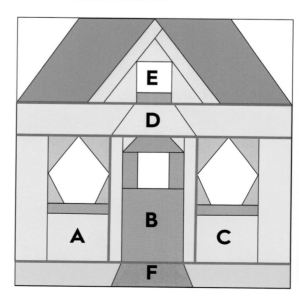

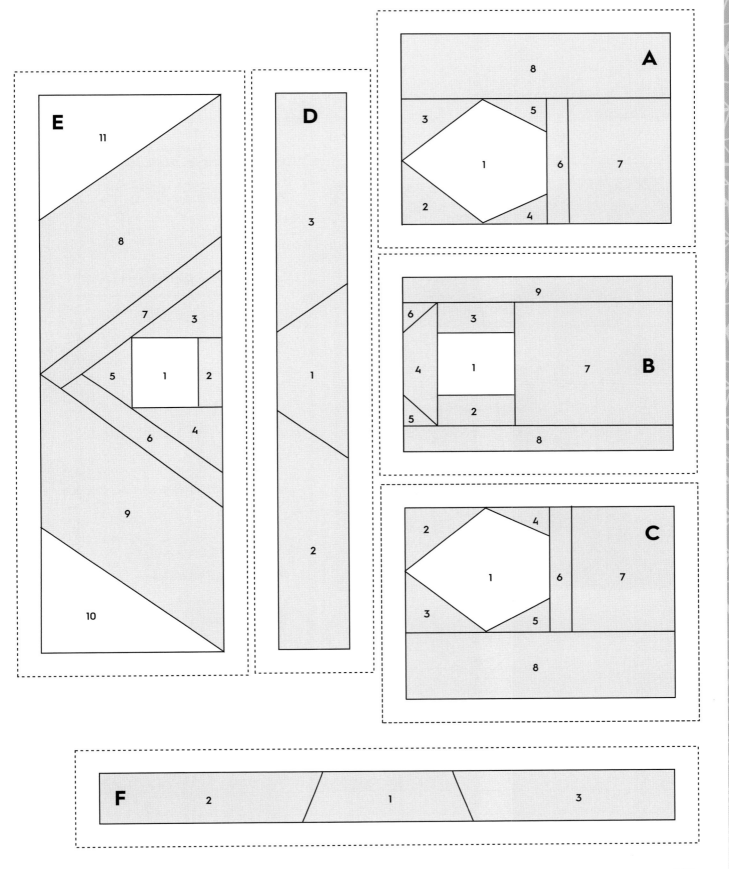

WINDMILL

Sarah Ashford

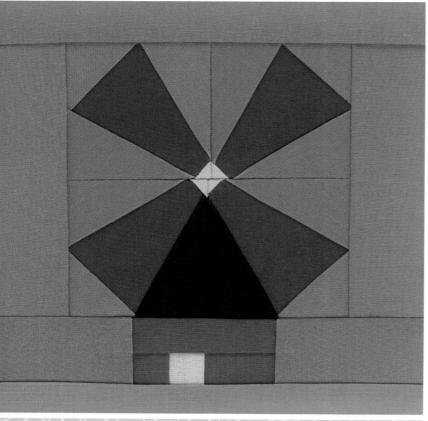

YOU WILL NEED

- Large scrap of bright blue fabric, at least 9" x 9" (23cm x 23cm)
- Large scrap of bright green fabric, at least 7" x 1½" (18cm x 4cm)
- Smaller scraps of red, yellow, dark blue and brown fabrics

BLOCK CONSTRUCTION

Make one copy each of patterns A, B, C, D, E, F, G and H.

Complete sections A to H.

Join B to C. Press seam open.

Join D to E. Press seam open.

Join BC to DE. Press seam open.

Join F and G to BCDE. Press seams towards F and G.

Join H to BCDEFG. Press seam towards H.

Join A to BCDEFGH. Press seam towards A.

REFERENCE DIAGRAM

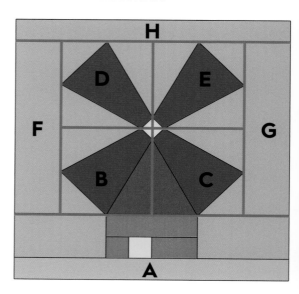

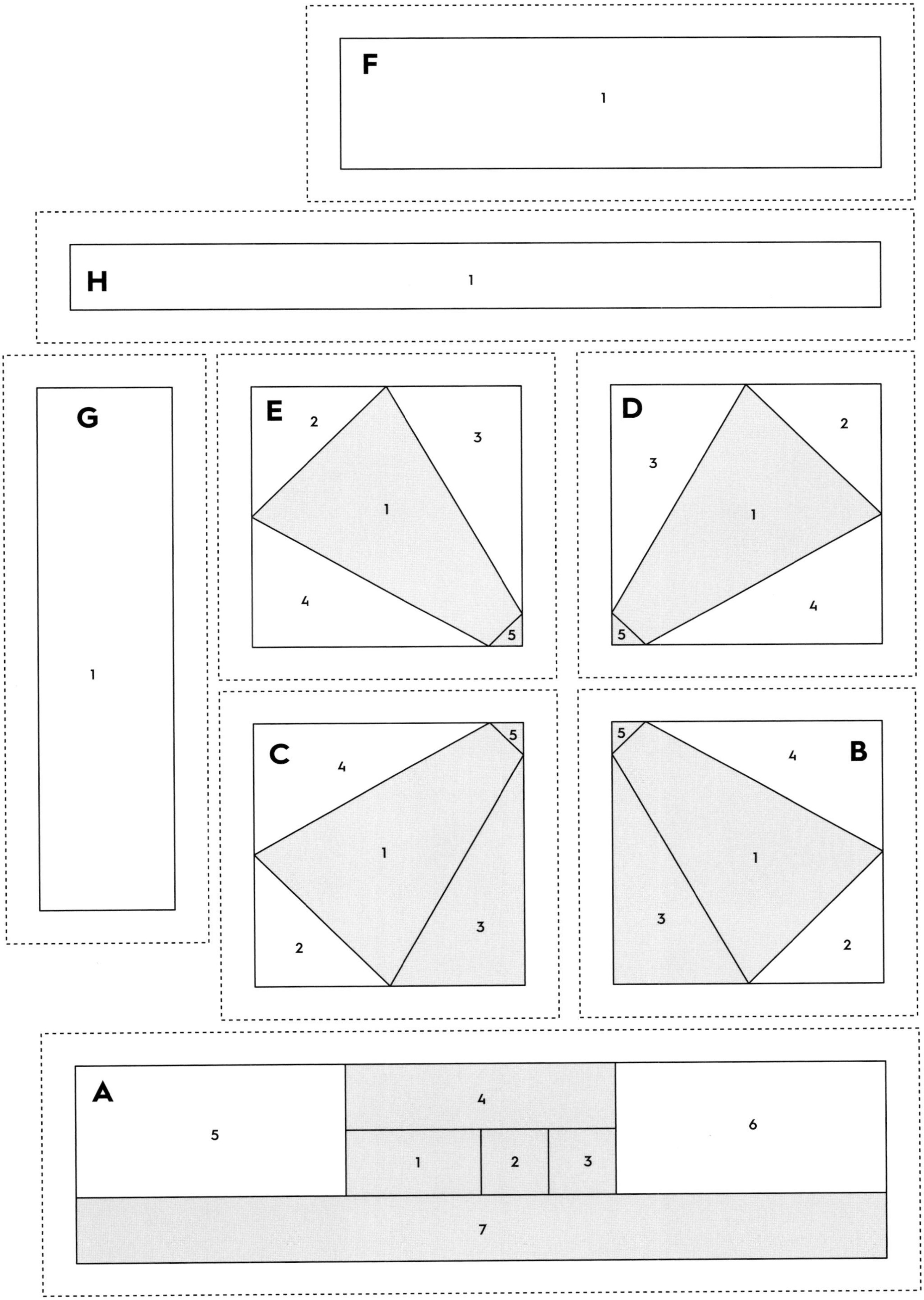

F

1

H

1

G

1

E

2

3

1

4

5

D

2

3

1

4

5

C

4

1

2

3

5

B

5

4

1

3

2

A

5

4

1   2   3

6

7

TENT

Susan White

YOU WILL NEED

- Large scrap of white fabric, at least 10" x 10" (25.5cm x 25.5cm)
- Large scrap of outdoors print fabric, at least 7" x 3" (18cm x 7.5cm)
- Smaller scraps of grey and assorted blue fabrics

BLOCK CONSTRUCTION

Make one copy of pattern A.

Complete section A.

REFERENCE DIAGRAM

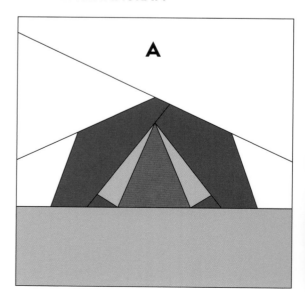

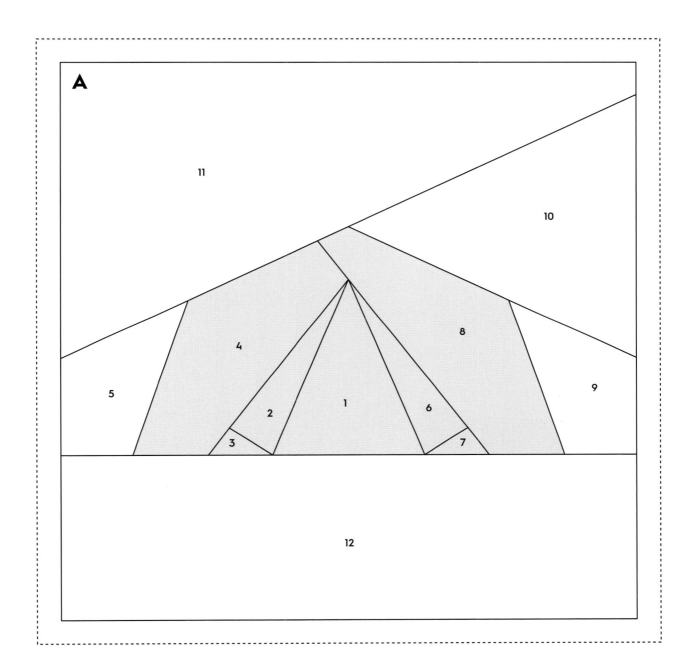

CAMPFIRE

Susan White

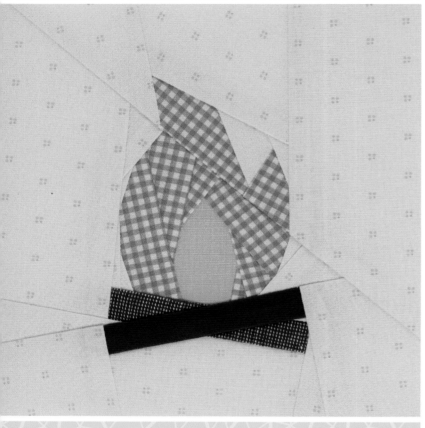

YOU WILL NEED

- One fat eighth of white/light print fabric
- Smaller scraps of orange gingham, yellow and assorted brown fabrics

BLOCK CONSTRUCTION

Make one copy each of patterns A, B and C.

Complete sections A to C.

Join A to B. Press seam towards A.

Join AB to C. Press seam towards C.

REFERENCE DIAGRAM

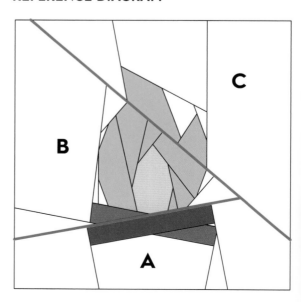

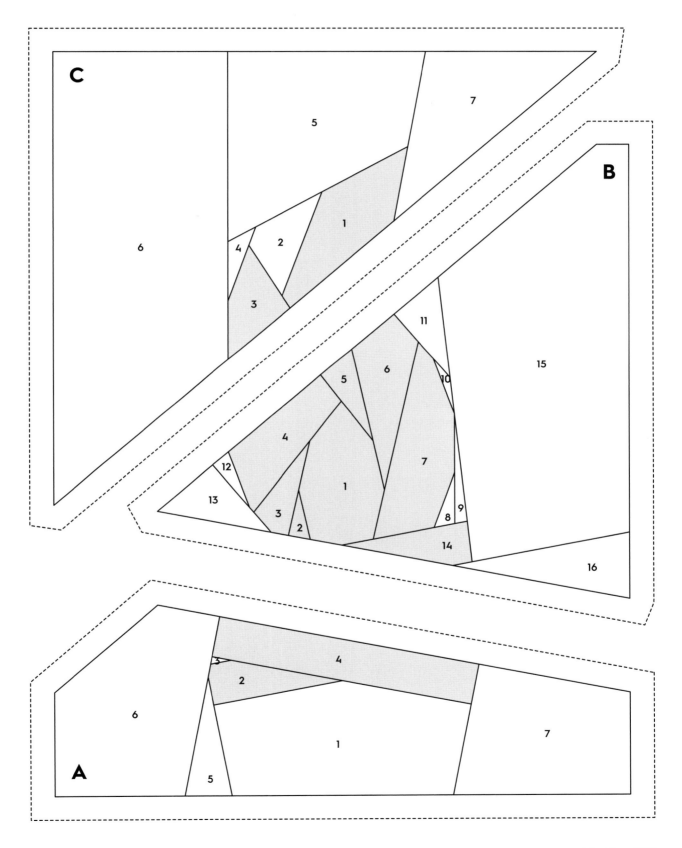

BEACH HUTS

Kerry Green

YOU WILL NEED

* Large scrap of blue fabric, at least 7" x 10" (18cm x 25.5cm)

* Large scrap of white fabric, at least 6" x 11" (15.5cm x 28cm)

* Large scrap of grey fabric, at least 5" x 10" (13cm x 25.5cm)

* Large scrap of sand fabric, at least 3" x 6½" (7.5cm x 16.5cm)

* Smaller scraps of mint, yellow and bright pink fabrics

BLOCK CONSTRUCTION

Make one copy each of patterns A, B, C, D and E.

Complete sections A to E.

Join A to B. Press seam open.

Join AB to C. Press seam open.

Join D to ABC. Press seam towards D.

Join E to ABCD. Press seam towards E.

REFERENCE DIAGRAM

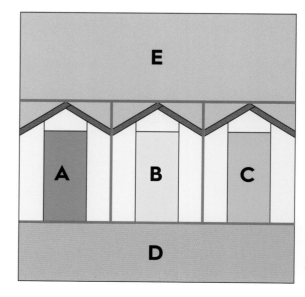

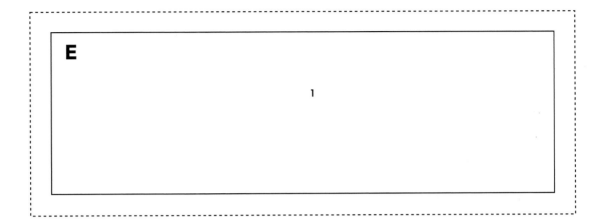

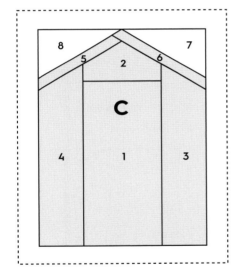

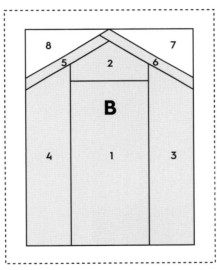

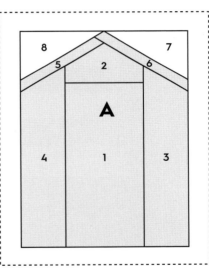

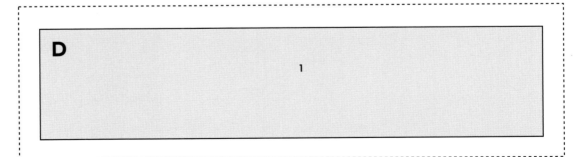

LIGHTHOUSE

Kitty Wilkin

YOU WILL NEED

* Large scrap of turquoise fabric, at least 8" x 10" (20.5cm x 25.5cm)
* Large scrap of red fabric, at least 6" x 3" (15.5cm x 7.5cm)
* Large scrap of dark blue fabric, at least 6" x 3" (15.5cm x 7.5cm)
* Smaller scraps of white, black, yellow and green fabrics

BLOCK CONSTRUCTION

Make one copy each of patterns A, B, C, D and E.

Complete sections A to E.

Join A to B. Press seam open.

Join AB to C. Press seam towards AB.

Join ABC to D. Press seam towards D.

Join ABCD to E. Press seam towards E.

REFERENCE DIAGRAM

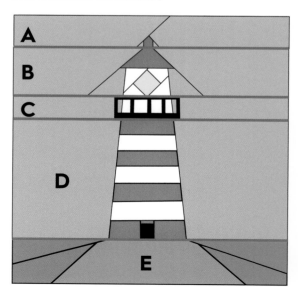

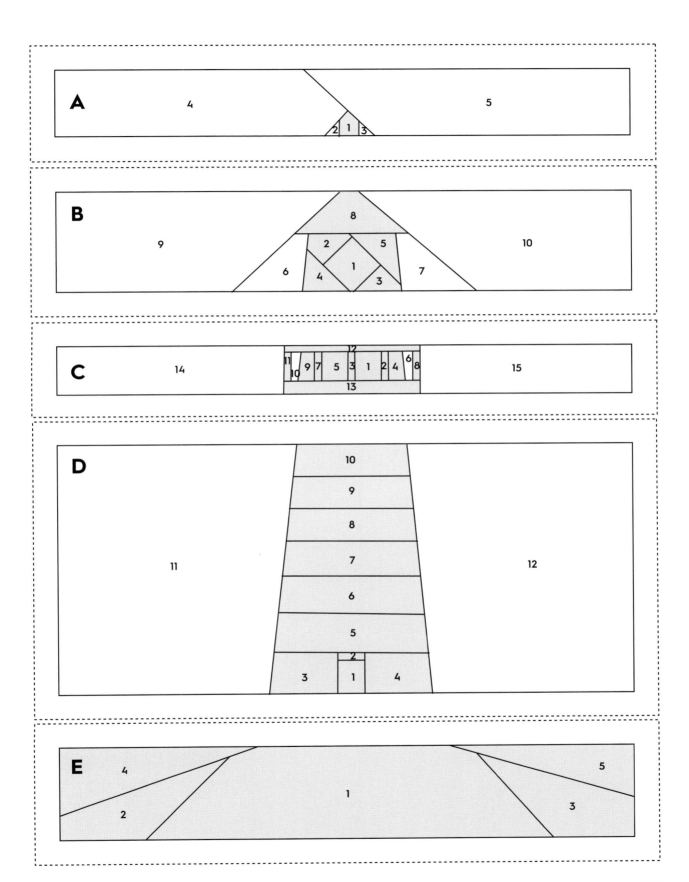

CANOE
Susan White

YOU WILL NEED

* One fat eighth of white fabric
* Smaller scraps of light green, mid green and light brown fabrics

BLOCK CONSTRUCTION

Make one copy each of patterns A, B and C.

Complete sections A to C.

Join A to B. Press seam towards B.

Join AB to C. Press seam towards C.

REFERENCE DIAGRAM

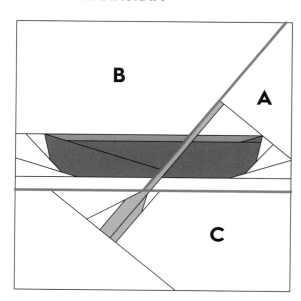

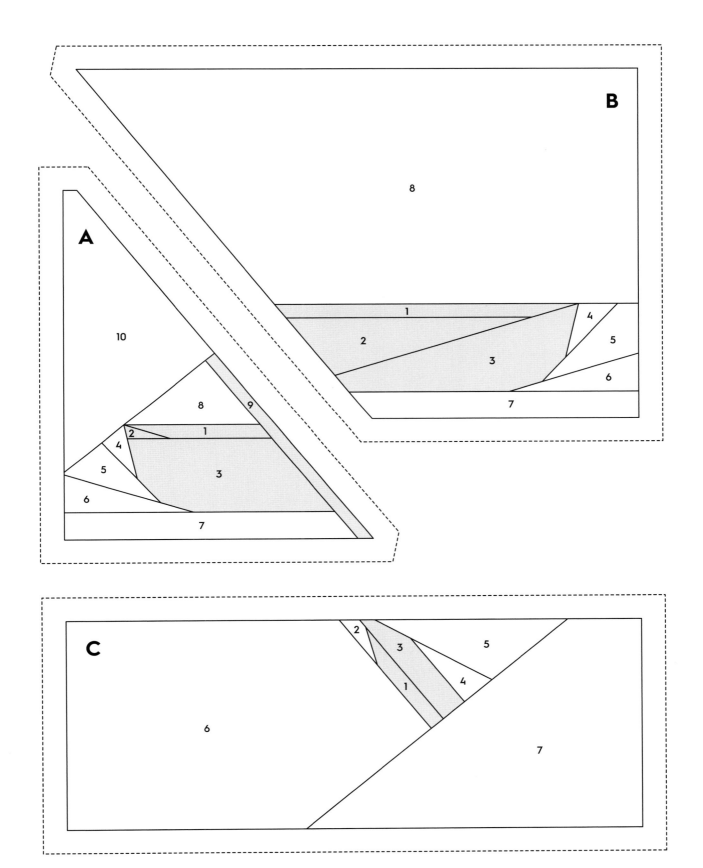

SAILBOAT

Kitty Wilkin

YOU WILL NEED

* Large scrap of turquoise fabric, at least 7" x 11" (18cm x 28cm)
* Smaller scraps of bright white and dark blue fabrics

BLOCK CONSTRUCTION

Make one copy each of patterns A and B.

Complete sections A to B.

Join A to B. Press seam open.

REFERENCE DIAGRAM

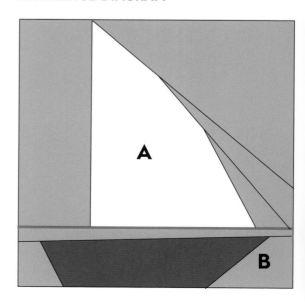

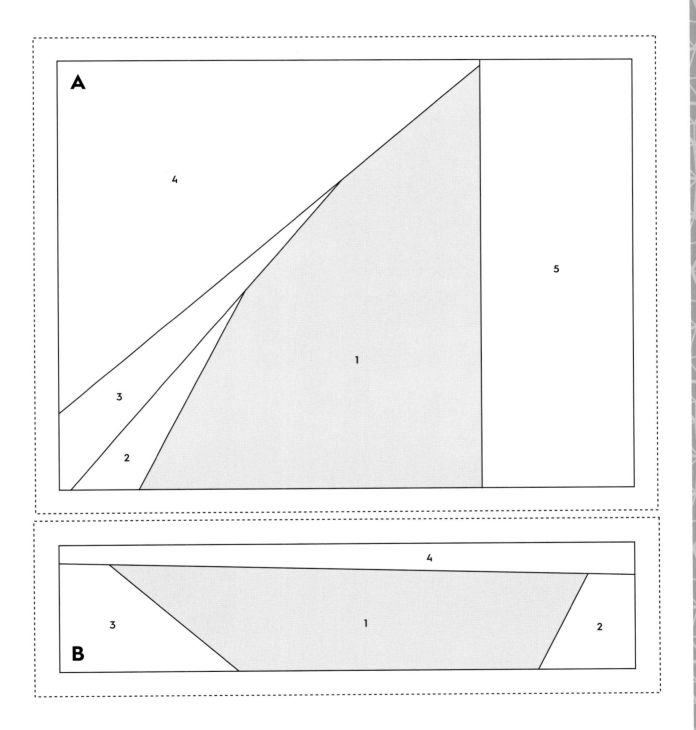

PALM TREE

Sarah Ashford

YOU WILL NEED

- One fat eighth of peach fabric
- Large scrap of green fabric, at least 9" x 4" (23cm x 10cm)
- Large scrap of brown fabric, at least 10" x 2" (25.5cm x 5cm)

BLOCK CONSTRUCTION

Make one copy each of patterns A, B and C.

Complete sections A to C.

Join B to C. Press seam open.

Join BC to A. Press seam towards A.

REFERENCE DIAGRAM

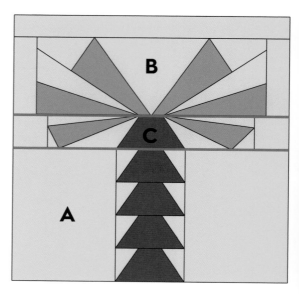

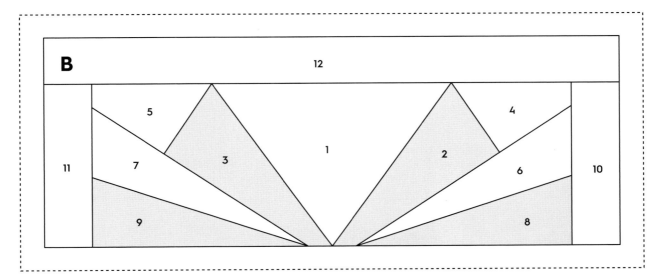

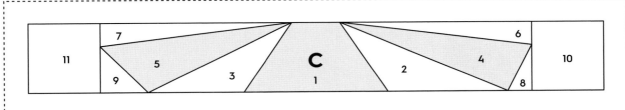

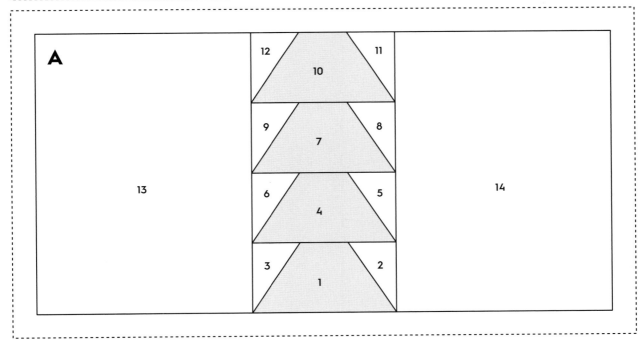

CACTUS
Joanne Hart

YOU WILL NEED

- One fat eighth of white/light print fabric
- Smaller scraps of bright leaf green, lime green, yellow green, light blue and black fabrics

BLOCK CONSTRUCTION

Make one copy each of patterns A, B, C and D.

Complete sections A to D.

Join A to B. Press seam towards B.

Join AB to C. Press seam towards AB.

Join ABC to D. Press seam open.

REFERENCE DIAGRAM

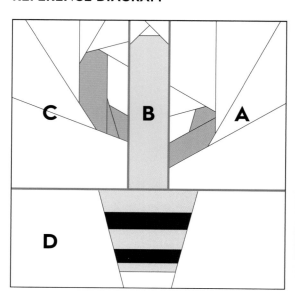

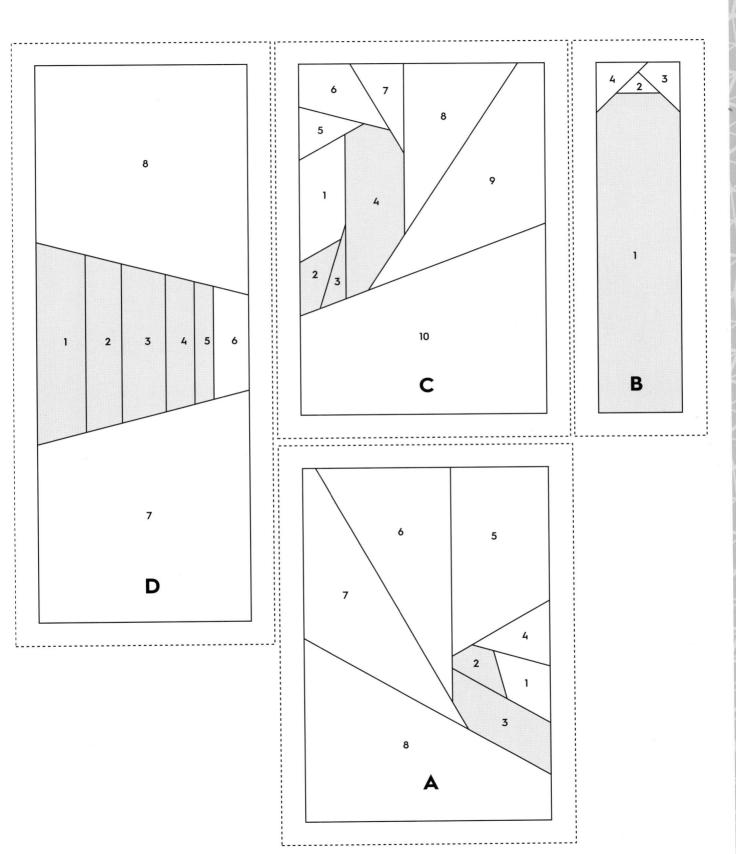

STRAWBERRY

Lindsay Chieco

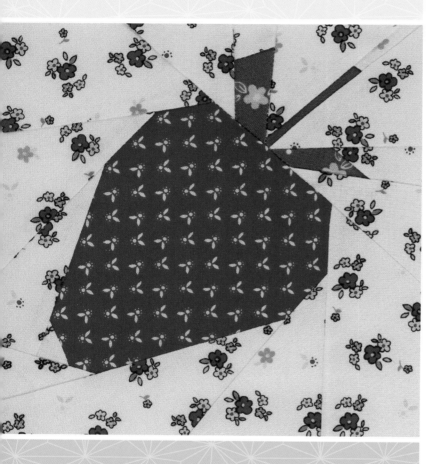

YOU WILL NEED

* Large scrap of white/light print fabric, at least 11" x 11" (28cm x 28cm)
* Smaller scraps of red and green fabrics

BLOCK CONSTRUCTION

Make one copy each of patterns A, B, C and D.

Complete sections A to D.

Join C to B. Press seam towards C.

Join CB to D. Press seam towards CB.

Join CBD to A. Press seam towards A.

REFERENCE DIAGRAM

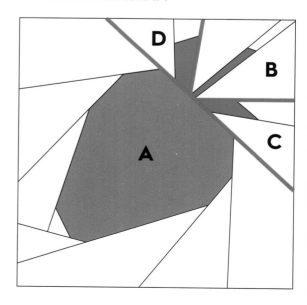

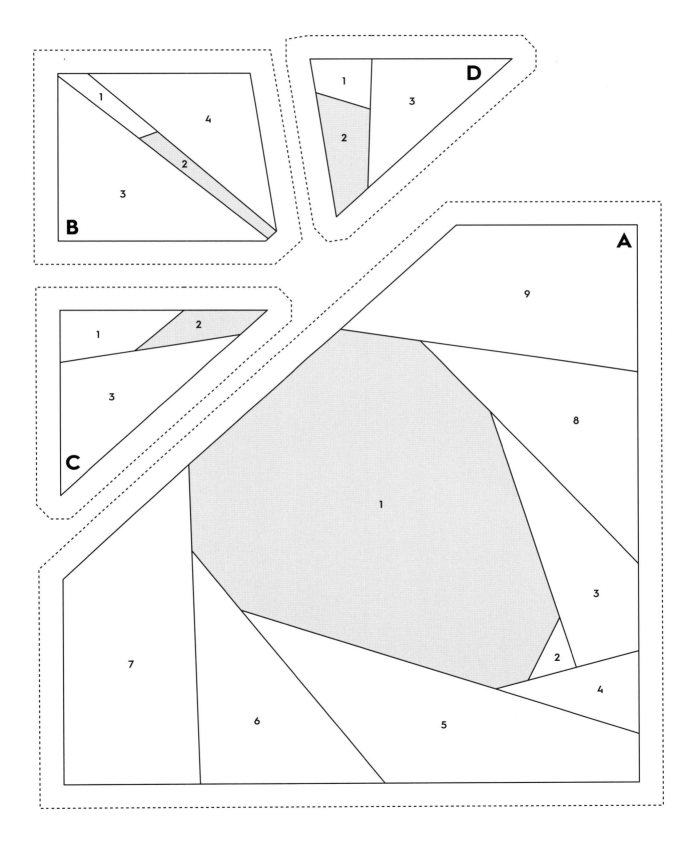

LEMON

Susan White

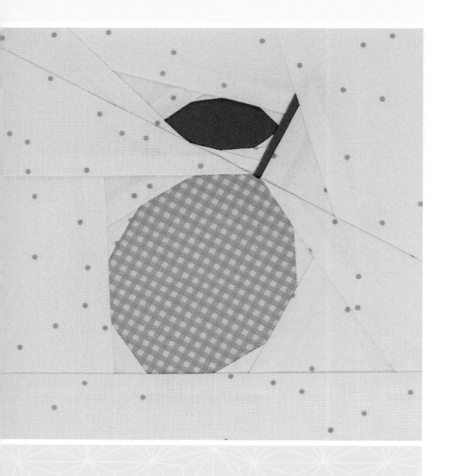

178

YOU WILL NEED

- One fat eighth of white/light print fabric
- Smaller scraps of yellow and bright green fabrics

BLOCK CONSTRUCTION

Make one copy each of patterns A and B.

Complete sections A and B.

Join A to B. Press seam towards B.

REFERENCE DIAGRAM

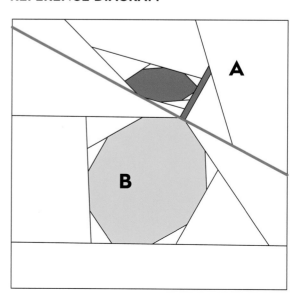

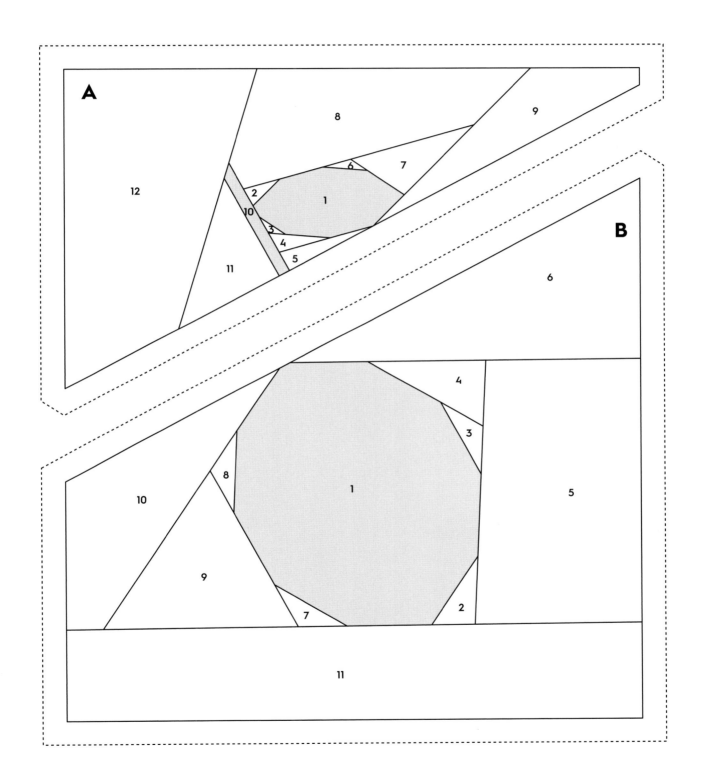

GRAPEFRUIT

Charise Randell

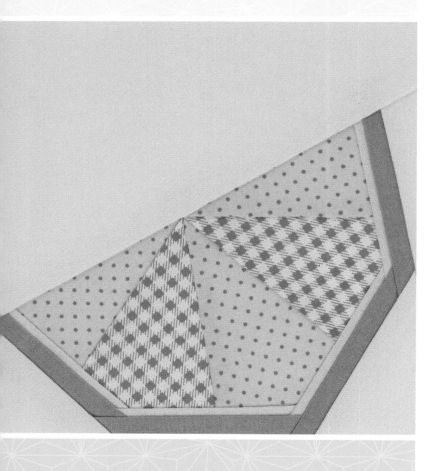

YOU WILL NEED

* Large scrap of white fabric, at least 10" x 10" (25.5cm x 25.5cm)

* Large scrap of pink dot fabric, at least 10" x 10" (25.5cm x 25.5cm)

* Large scrap of pink gingham fabric, at least 10" x 10" (25.5cm x 25.5cm)

* Smaller scraps of salmon pink and pale yellow fabrics

BLOCK CONSTRUCTION

Make one copy of pattern A.

Complete section A.

REFERENCE DIAGRAM

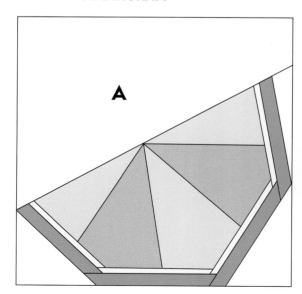

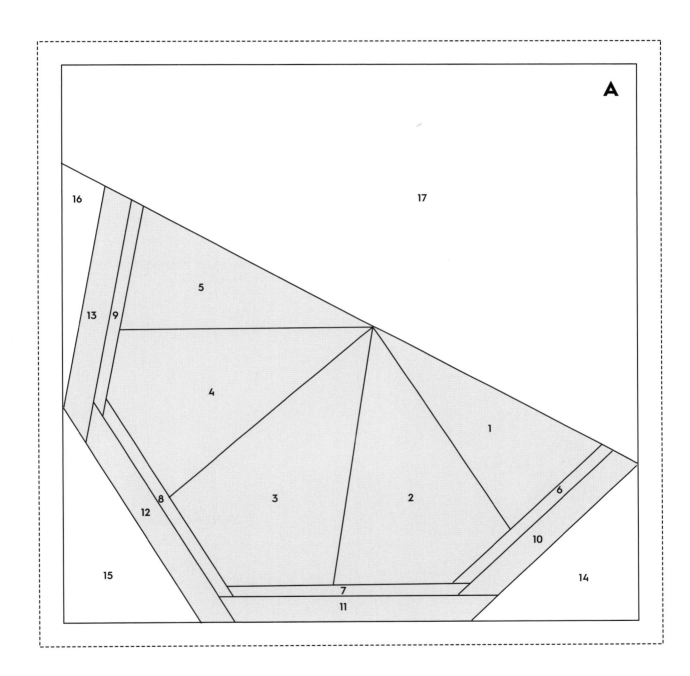

PINEAPPLE

Kristy Lea

YOU WILL NEED

* One fat eighth of white/light print fabric
* Smaller scraps of assorted yellow and green fabrics

BLOCK CONSTRUCTION

Make one copy of patterns A and B.

Complete sections A and B.

Join A to B. Press seam towards B.

REFERENCE DIAGRAM

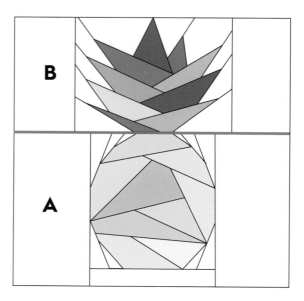

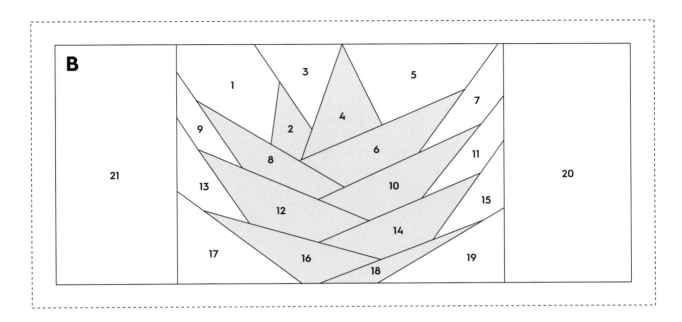

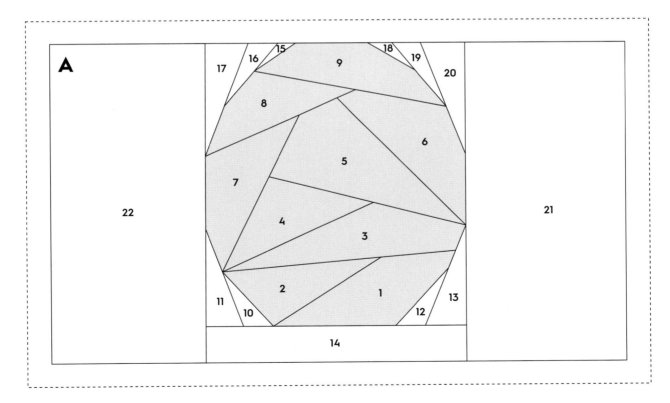

APPLE
Susan White

YOU WILL NEED

- One fat eighth of white/light print fabric
- Smaller scraps of light pink and leaf green fabrics

BLOCK CONSTRUCTION

Make one copy each of patterns A, B and C.

Complete sections A to C.

Join A to B. Press seam towards B.

Join AB to C. Press seam towards C.

REFERENCE DIAGRAM

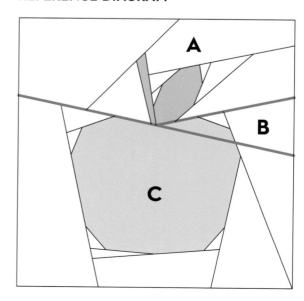

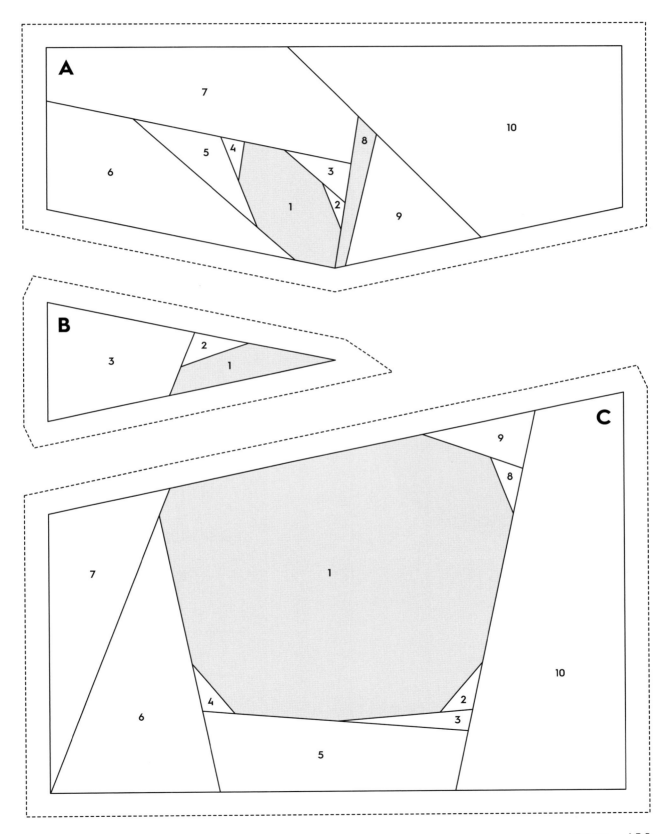

PEAR

Lindsay Chieco

YOU WILL NEED

* Large scrap of white/light print fabric, at least 11" x 11" (28cm x 28cm)
* Smaller scraps of light green, dark green and brown fabrics

BLOCK CONSTRUCTION

Make one copy each of patterns A, B, C and D.

Complete sections A to D.

Join D to C. Press seam towards D.

Join DC to B. Press seam towards B.

Join DCB to A. Press seam towards A.

REFERENCE DIAGRAM

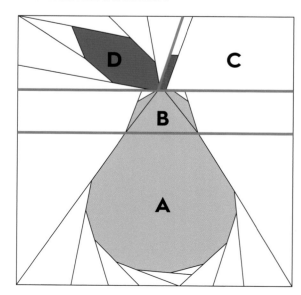

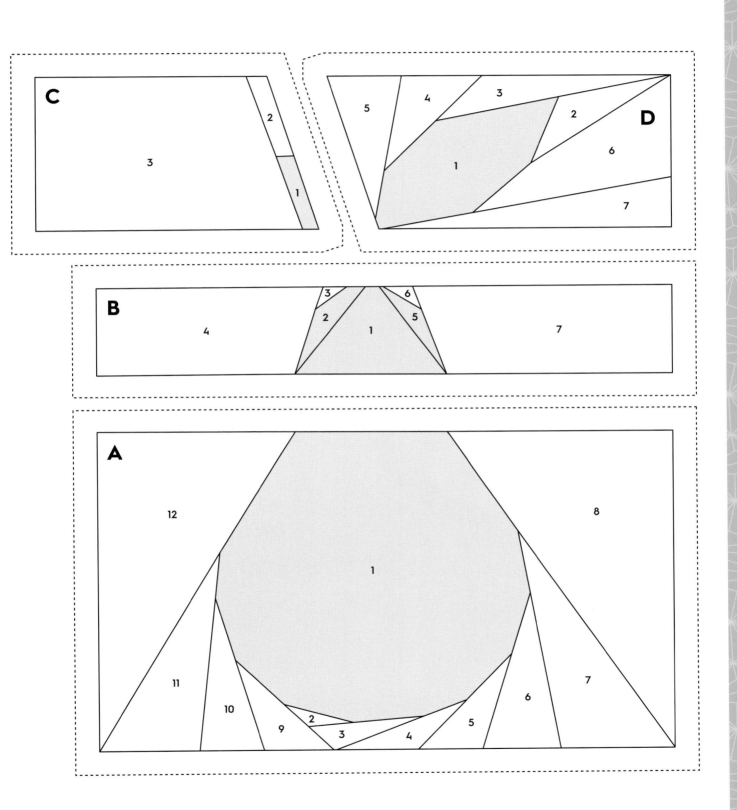

WATERMELON

Lindsay Chicco

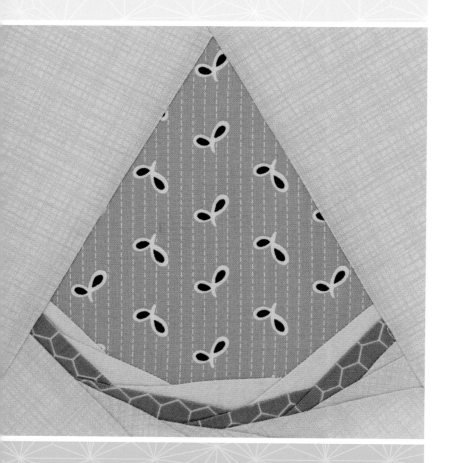

YOU WILL NEED

- Large scrap of pale green fabric, at least 11" x 11" (28cm x 28cm)
- Smaller scraps of pink, cream and mid green fabrics

BLOCK CONSTRUCTION

Make one copy of pattern A.

Complete section A.

REFERENCE DIAGRAM

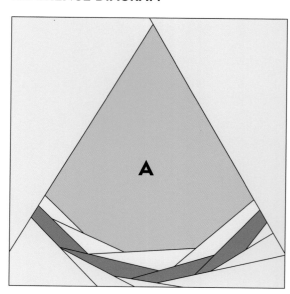

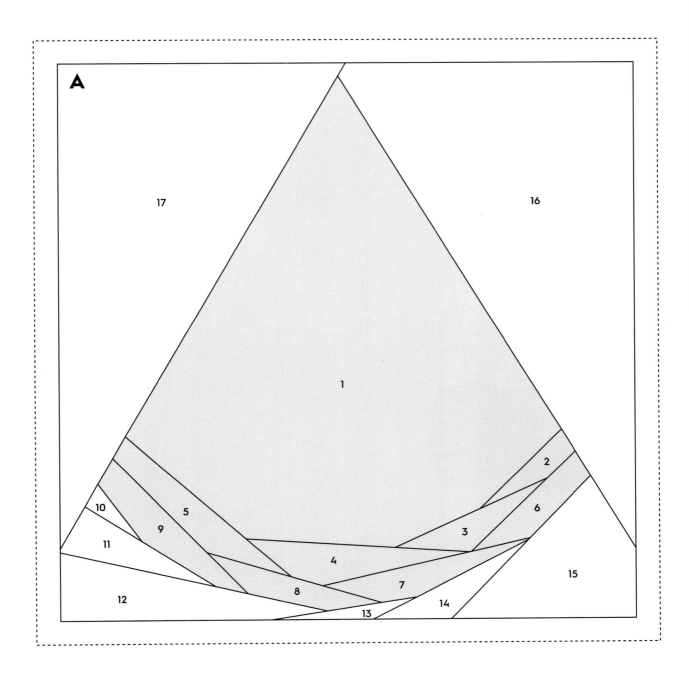

CHERRY

Susan White

YOU WILL NEED

- One fat eighth of white/light print fabric
- Smaller scraps of bright cherry red and bright green fabrics

BLOCK CONSTRUCTION

Make one copy each of patterns A, B and C.

Complete sections A to C.

Join A to B. Press seam towards B.

Join AB to C. Press seam towards C.

REFERENCE DIAGRAM

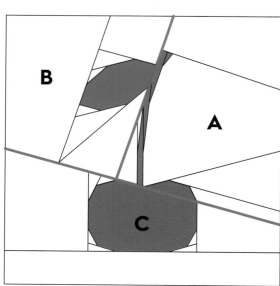

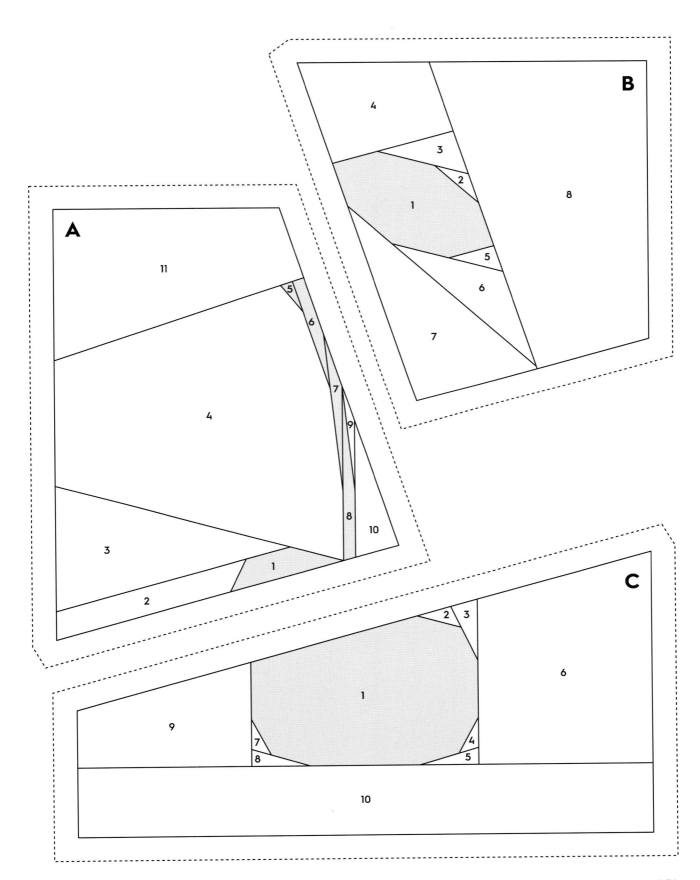

SEWING MACHINE

Charise Randell

YOU WILL NEED

- One fat eighth of white fabric
- Large scraps of blue and yellow fabric, each at least 10" x 10" (25.5cm x 25.5cm)
- Smaller scraps of yellow, pink, brown and dark grey fabrics

BLOCK CONSTRUCTION

Make one copy each of patterns A, B, C, D, E, F, G and H.

Complete sections A to H.

Join A to B. Press seam towards A.

Join C to AB. Press seam towards AB.

Join D to ABC. Press seam towards D.

Join E to ABCD. Press seam towards E.

Join F to ABCDE. Press seam towards F.

Join G to ABCDEF. Press seam towards ABCDEF.

Join H to ABCDEFG. Press seam towards H.

REFERENCE DIAGRAM

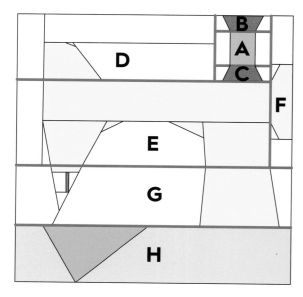

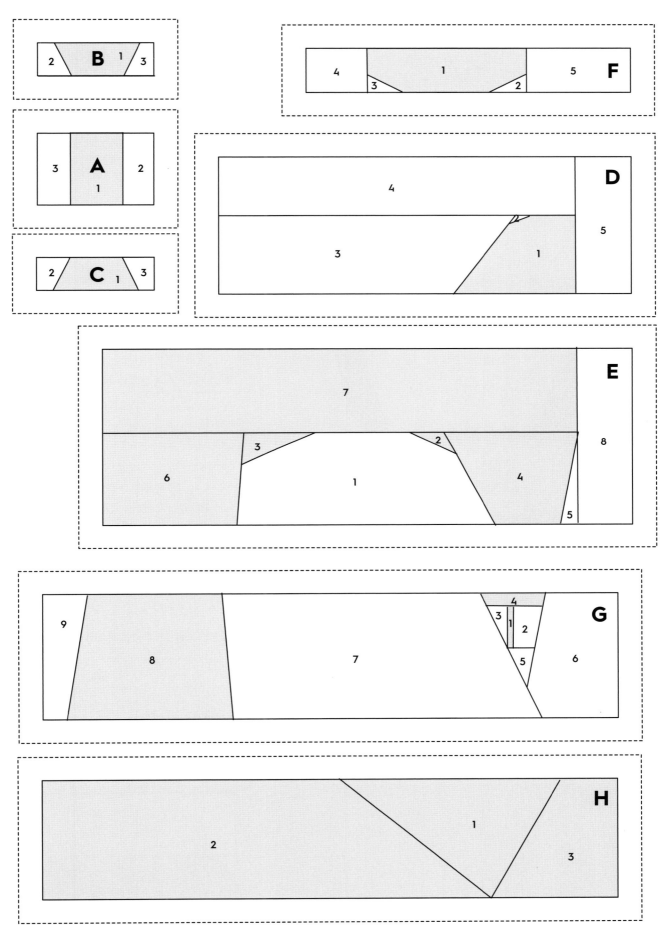

VINTAGE IRON

Charise Randell

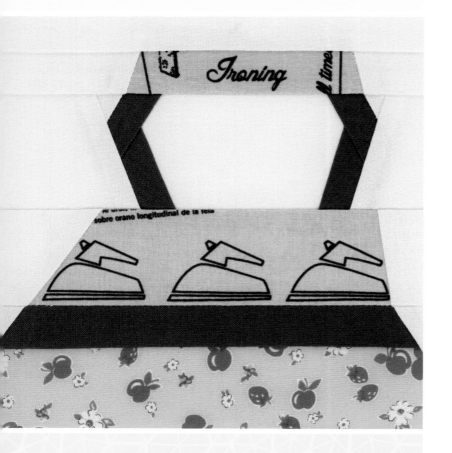

YOU WILL NEED

- Large scrap of white fabric, at least 10" x 10" (25.5cm x 25.5cm)
- Large scrap of grey fabric, at least 10" x 10" (25.5cm x 25.5cm)
- Large scrap of blue fabric, at least 4" x 6½" (10cm x 16.5cm)
- Large scrap of yellow fabric, at least 4½" x 7½" (11.5cm x 19cm)

BLOCK CONSTRUCTION

Make one copy each of patterns A, B, C and D.

Complete sections A to D.

Join A to B. Press seam towards A.

Join C to AB. Press seam towards C.

Join D to ABC. Press seam open.

REFERENCE DIAGRAM

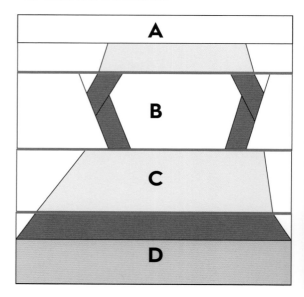

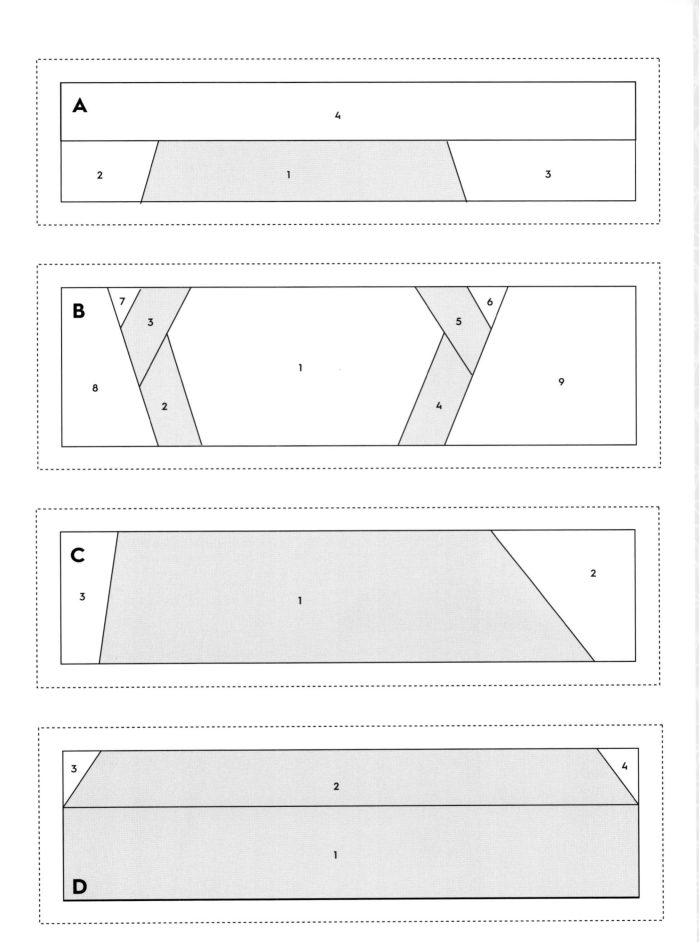

THREAD SPOOL

Charise Randell

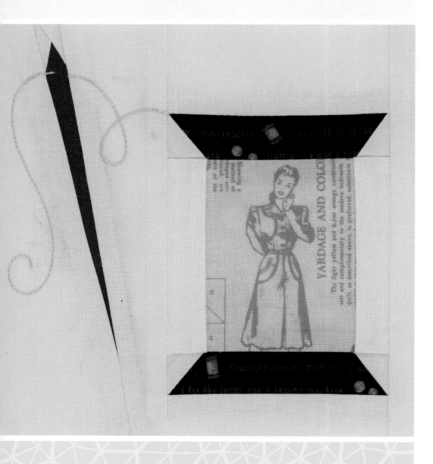

YOU WILL NEED

- Large scrap of white fabric, at least 10" x 10" (25.5cm x 25.5cm)
- Large scrap of grey fabric, at least 1½" x 6" (4cm x 15.5cm)
- Smaller scraps of pink and brown fabrics
- Pink embroidery thread

BLOCK CONSTRUCTION

Make one copy each of patterns A, B, C, D and E.

Complete sections A to E.

Join A to B. Press seam towards B.

Join C to AB. Press seam towards AB.

Join D to ABC. Press seam towards D.

Join E to ABCD. Press seam towards E.

Referring to the reference diagram, use a heat-erasable pen to draw the 'thread' through the needle. Lay unstranded embroidery thread on the marked line and couch with a single strand of thread (see General Techniques).

REFERENCE DIAGRAM

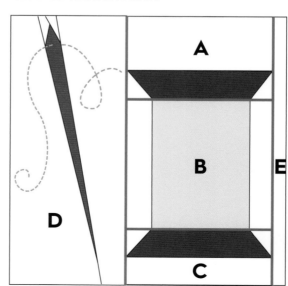

E

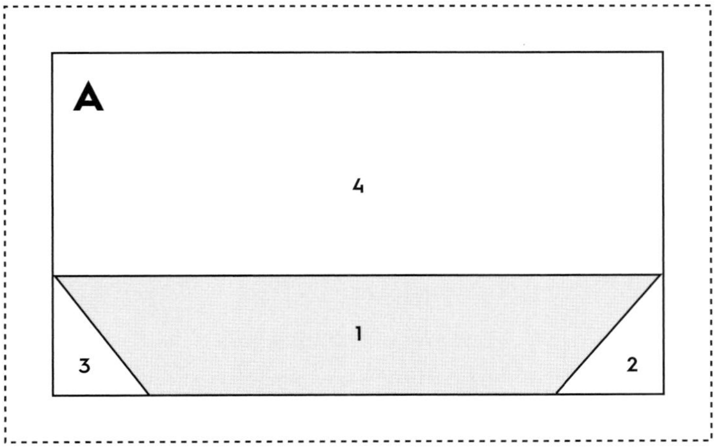

1

A

4

1

3   2

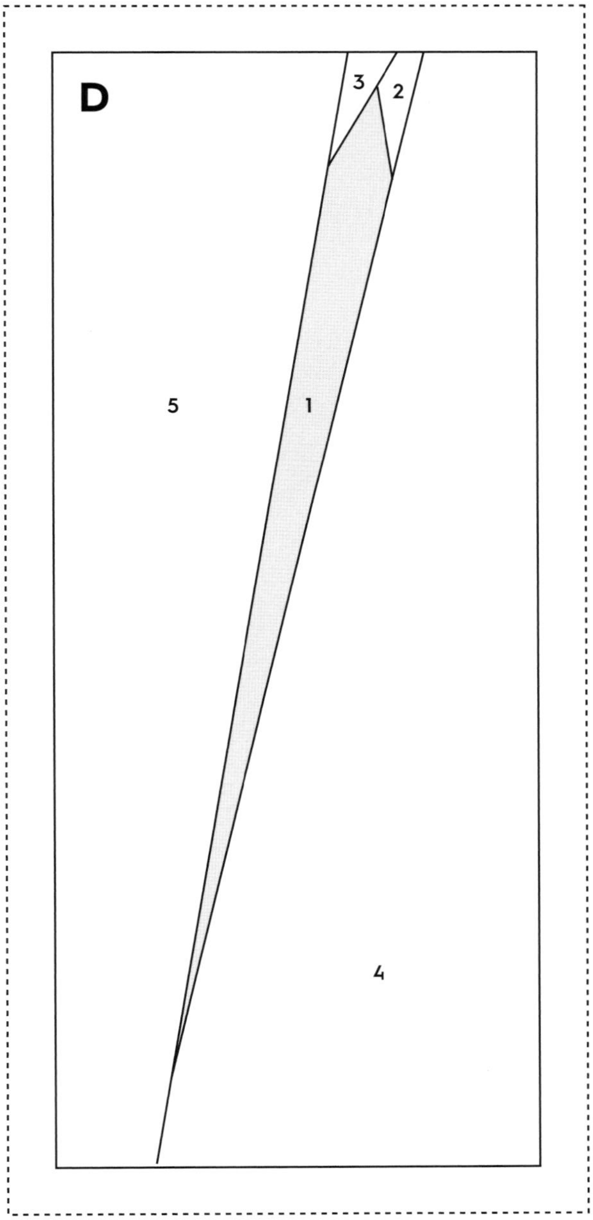

B

3   1   2

C

3   1   2

4

D

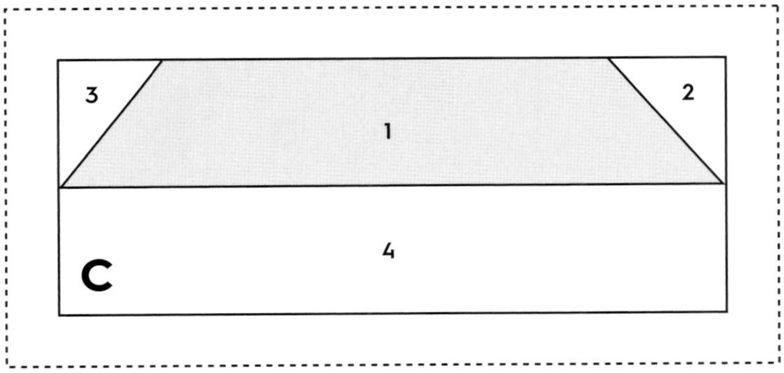

3 2

5   1

4

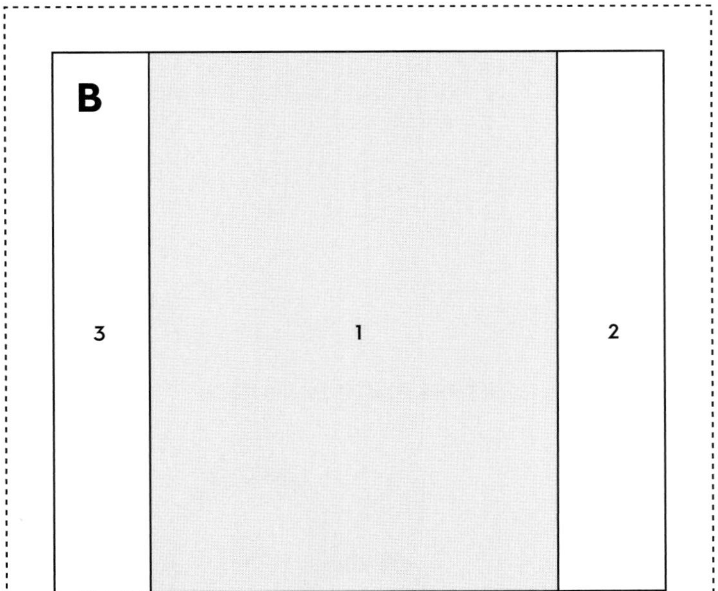

SCISSORS

Charise Randell

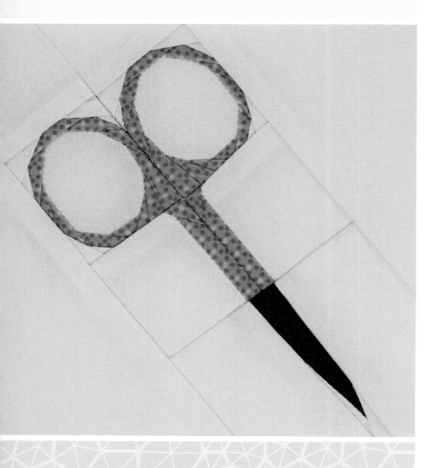

YOU WILL NEED

* One fat eighth of white fabric
* Large scrap of blue fabric, at least 10" x 10" (25.5cm x 25.5cm)
* Smaller scrap of dark grey fabric

BLOCK CONSTRUCTION

Make one copy each of patterns A, B, C, D, E, F and G.

Complete sections A to G.

Join A to B. Press seam towards B.

Join C to D. Press seam towards D.

Join AB to CD. Press seam open.

Join ABCD to E. Press seam towards E.

Join F and G to ABCDE. Press seams towards F and G.

REFERENCE DIAGRAM

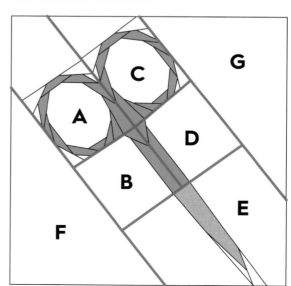

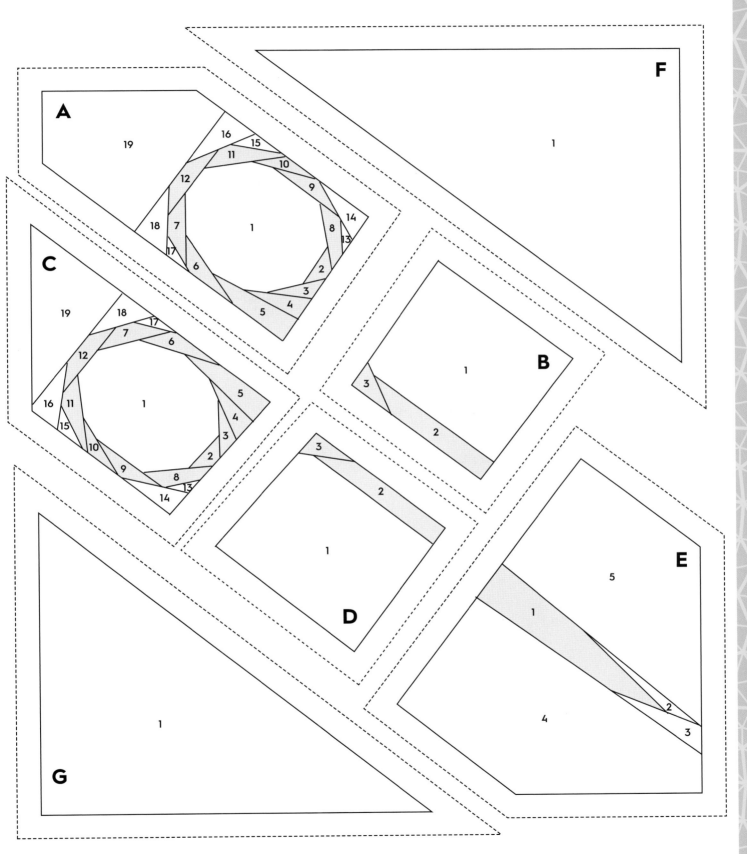

BOOK
Monika Henry

YOU WILL NEED

- Large scrap of white fabric, at least 7" x 10" (18cm x 25.5cm)

- Large scrap of cream print fabric, at least 3" x 4½" (8cm x 11.5cm), fussy cut for book cover

- Smaller scraps of mink, cream* and red* fabrics (*to coordinate with your chosen cream print fabric)

BLOCK CONSTRUCTION

Make one copy each of patterns A, B, C, D and E.

Complete sections A to E.

Join C to B. Press seam towards B.

Join BC to A. Press seam towards BC.

Join D to ABC. Press seam towards D.

Join E to ABCD. Press seam towards E.

REFERENCE DIAGRAM

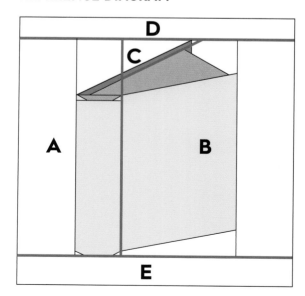

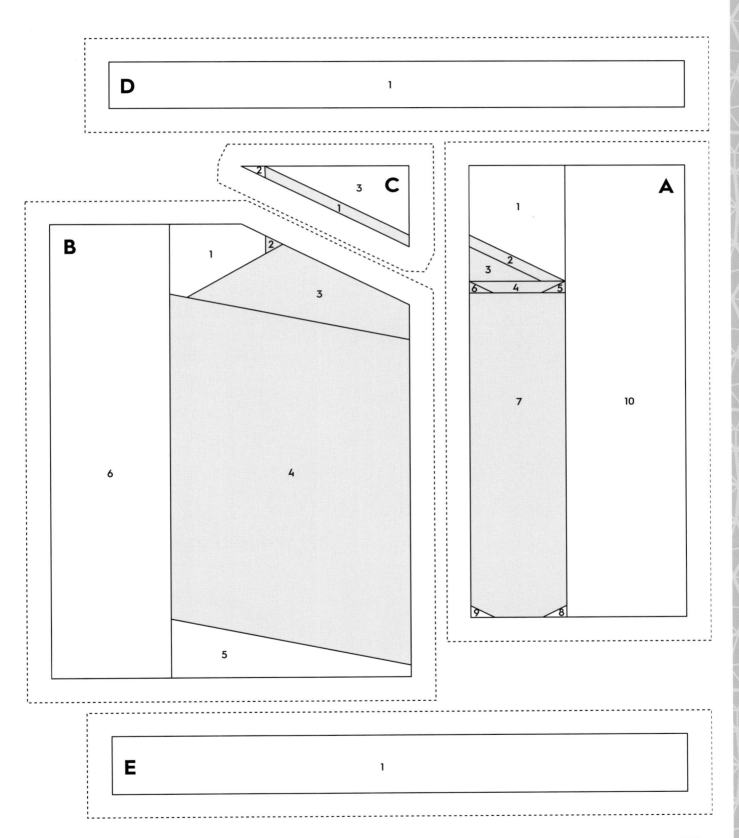

RADIO

Kerry Green

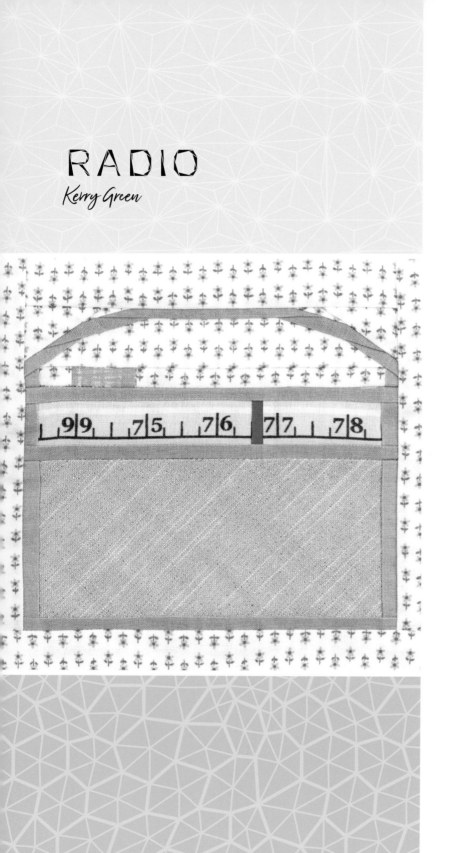

YOU WILL NEED

- Large scrap of white/light print fabric, at least 9" x 15" (23cm x 38cm)
- Large scrap of dark cream fabric, at least 3¼" x 5¾" (9cm x 15cm)
- Smaller scraps of cream number-print, light blue, grey and red fabrics

BLOCK CONSTRUCTION

Make one copy each of patterns A, B, C, D, E and F.

Complete sections A to F.

Join A to B. Press seam open.

Join AB to C. Press seam open.

Join D and E to ABC. Press seams towards D and E.

Join F to ABCDE. Press seam towards F.

REFERENCE DIAGRAM

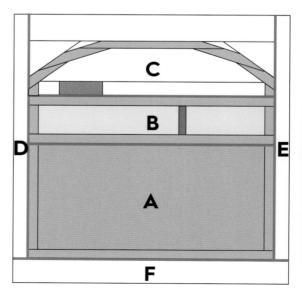

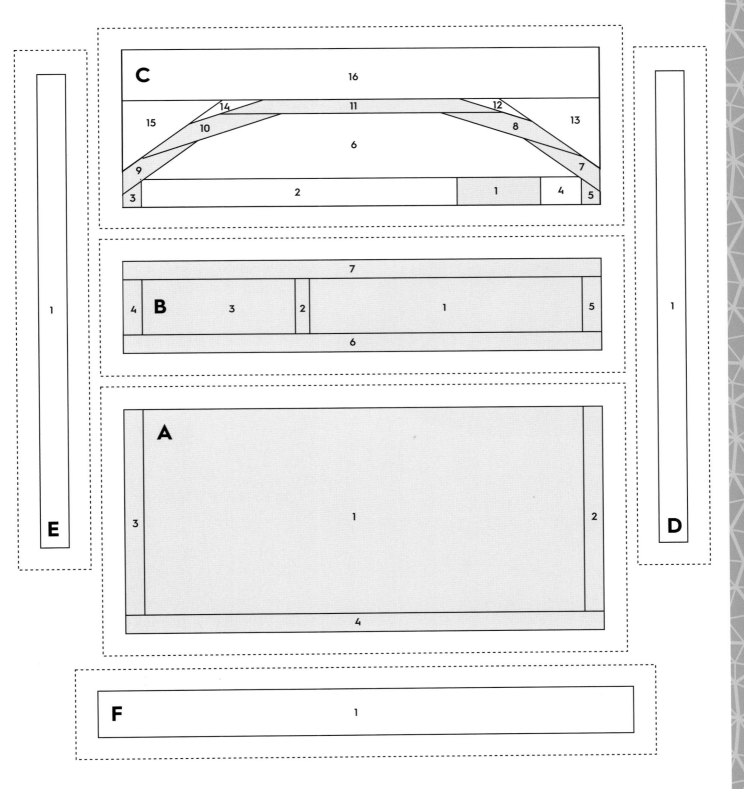

HAT
Charise Randell

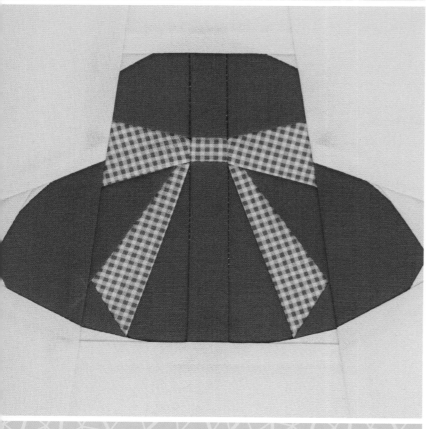

YOU WILL NEED

* Large scrap of white fabric, at least 10" x 10" (25.5cm x 25.5cm)
* Large scrap of fuchsia pink fabric, at least 10" x 10" (25.5cm x 25.5cm)
* Large scrap of pink gingham fabric, at least 10" x 10" (25.5cm x 25.5cm)

BLOCK CONSTRUCTION

Make one copy each of patterns A, B, C, D, E, F and G.

Complete sections A to G.

Join A to B. Press seam towards B.

Join C to AB. Press seam towards AB.

Join D to ABC. Press seam towards D.

Join E to ABCD. Press seam towards E.

Join F to ABCDE. Press seam towards F.

Join G to ABCDEF. Press seam towards G.

REFERENCE DIAGRAM

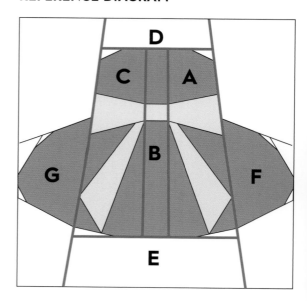

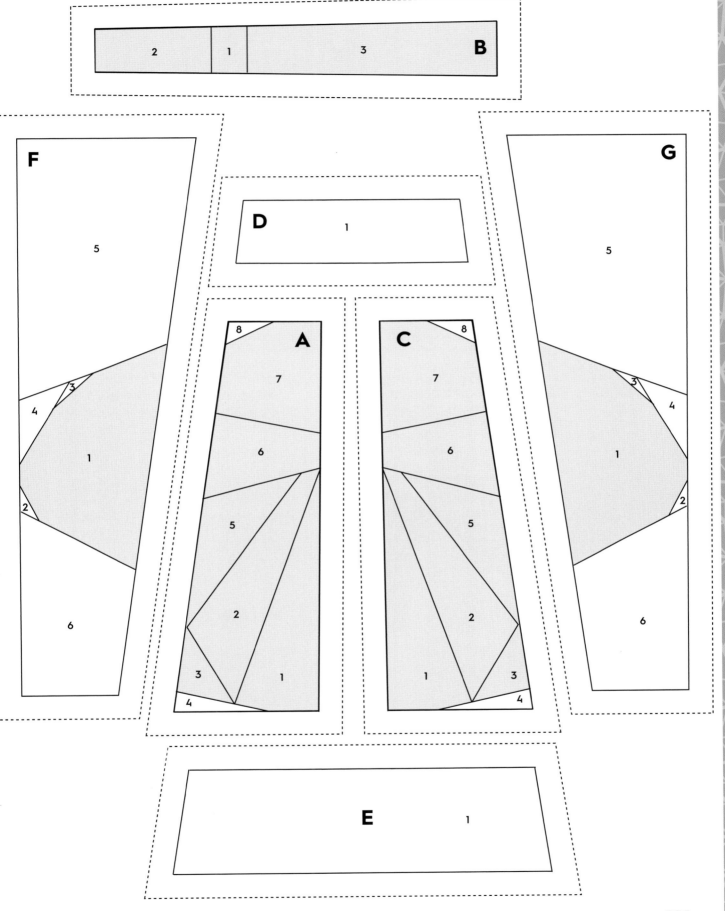

HIGH HEELS

Charise Randell

YOU WILL NEED

- One fat eighth of white fabric
- Large scrap of fuchsia pink fabric, at least 10" x 10" (25.5cm x 25.5cm)
- Large scrap of pink gingham fabric, at least 10" x 10" (25.5cm x 25.5cm)

BLOCK CONSTRUCTION

Make one copy each of patterns A, B, and C.

Complete sections A to C.

Join A to B. Press seam towards A.

Join C to AB. Press seam towards AB.

REFERENCE DIAGRAM

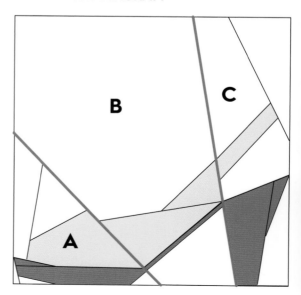

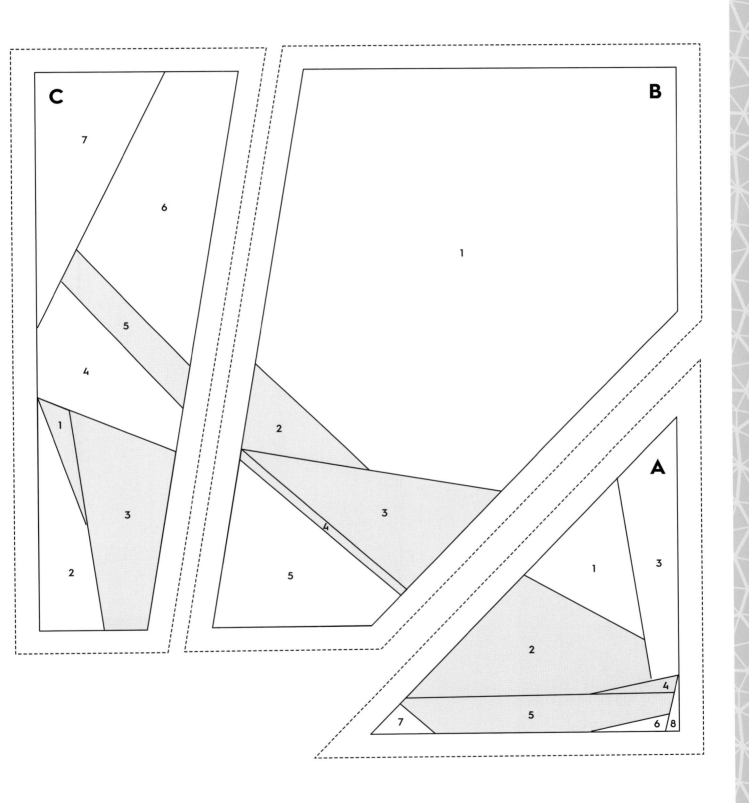

PURSE

Charise Randell

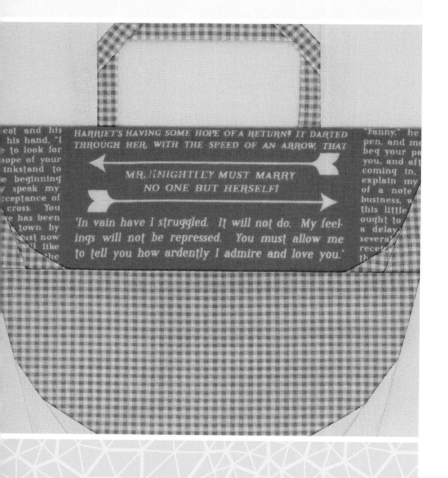

YOU WILL NEED

- Large scrap of white fabric, at least 10" x 10" (25.5cm x 25.5cm)
- Large scrap of aqua fabric, at least 7½" x 3¼" (19cm x 8.5cm)
- Large scrap of aqua gingham fabric, at least 10" x 10" (25.5cm x 25.5cm)

BLOCK CONSTRUCTION

Make one copy of pattern A.

Complete section A.

REFERENCE DIAGRAM

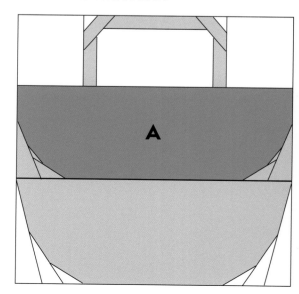

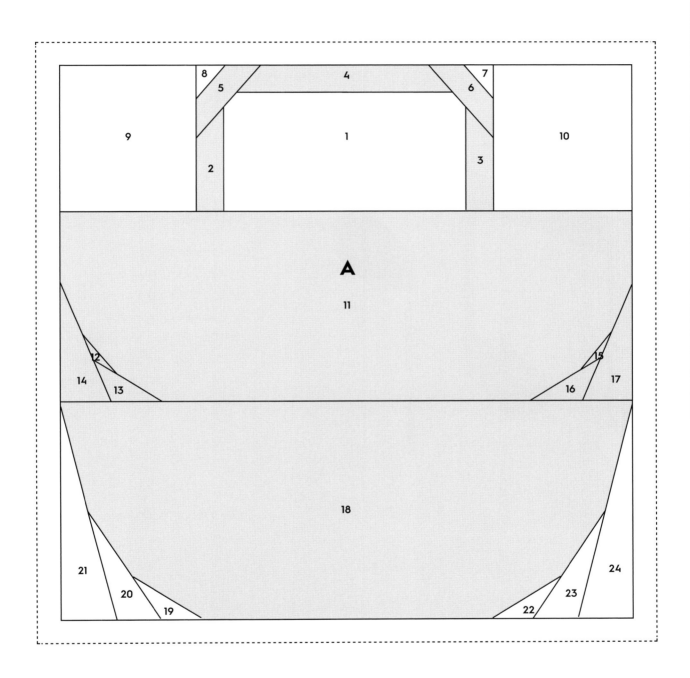

MUSIC NOTES

Kerry Green

YOU WILL NEED

- Large scrap of cream fabric, at least 16" x 19" (40.5cm x 48.5cm)
- Large scrap of black fabric, at least 9" x 9" (23cm x 23cm)

BLOCK CONSTRUCTION

Make one copy each of patterns A, B, C, D, E, F and G.

Complete sections A to G.

Join A to B. Press seam open.

Join C to D. Press seam open.

Join E to F. Press seam open.

Join CD to EF. Press seam open.

Join CDEF to G. Press seam open.

Join AB to CDEFG. Press seam open.

REFERENCE DIAGRAM

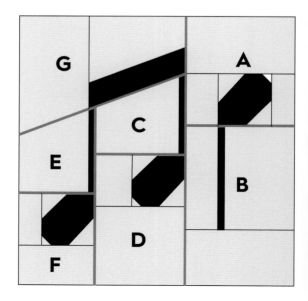

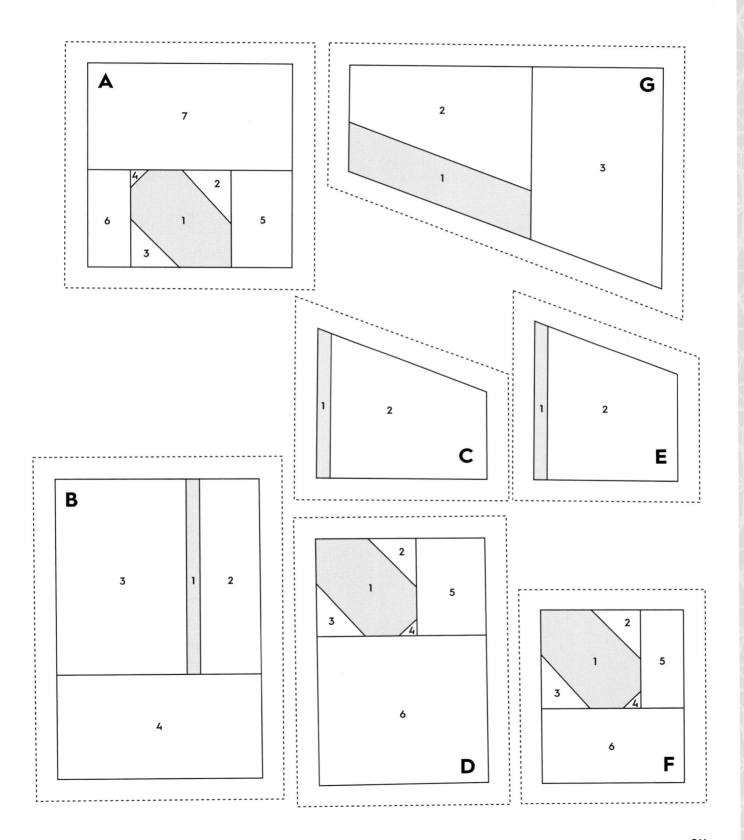

CAMERA

Charise Randell

YOU WILL NEED

* Large scraps of aqua gingham and white fabrics, each at least 7" x 5" (18cm x 13cm)
* Large scraps of bright aqua and white floral fabrics, each at least 5" x 10" (13cm x 25.5cm)
* Smaller scraps of bright aqua print, grey and white city print (lens) fabrics

BLOCK CONSTRUCTION

Make one copy each of patterns A, B, C, D, E, F, G and H.

Complete sections A to H.

Join A to B. Press seam towards A.

Join C to AB. Press seam towards C.

Join D to E. Press seam open.

Join DE to F. Press seam open.

Join ABC to DEF. Press seam towards DEF.

Join G to ABCDEF. Press seam towards G.

Join H to ABCDEFG. Press seam towards H.

Using the lens patterns and following Making a Circle Appliqué (see General Techniques), make a large (aqua) and small (white) circle appliqué. Sew in place (see dashed lines on reference diagram).

REFERENCE DIAGRAM

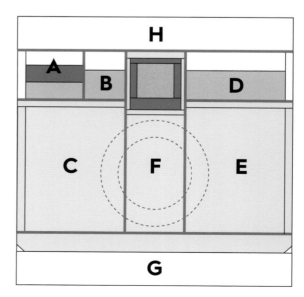

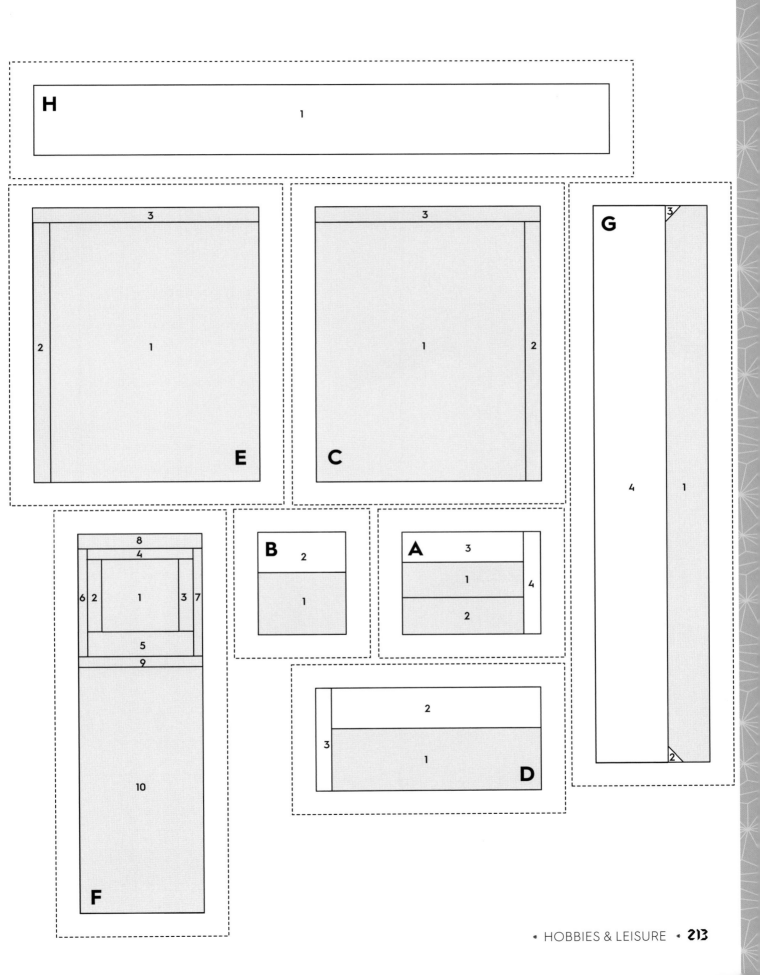

RETRO PHONE

Charise Randell

YOU WILL NEED

* One fat eighth of white fabric
* Large scrap of peach polka dot fabric, at least 10" x 10" (25.5cm x 25.5cm)
* Smaller scraps of peach, grey and retro phone dial print (or white) fabrics

BLOCK CONSTRUCTION

Make one copy each of patterns A, B, C, D, E, F and G.

Complete sections A to G.

Join A to B. Press seam towards B.

Join C to D. Press seam towards D.

Join AB and CD to E. Press seams towards E.

Join ABCDE to F. Press seam towards F.

Join ABCDEF to G. Press seam towards G.

Using the dial pattern and following Making a Circle Appliqué (see General Techniques), make a circle appliqué: dial-print fabric has been used here but you could use white fabric and draw on a dial design with fabric markers. Sew in place (see dashed lines on reference diagram).

REFERENCE DIAGRAM

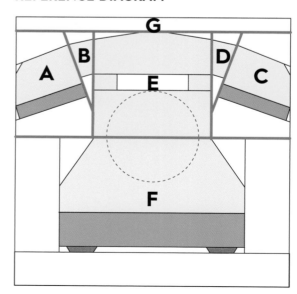

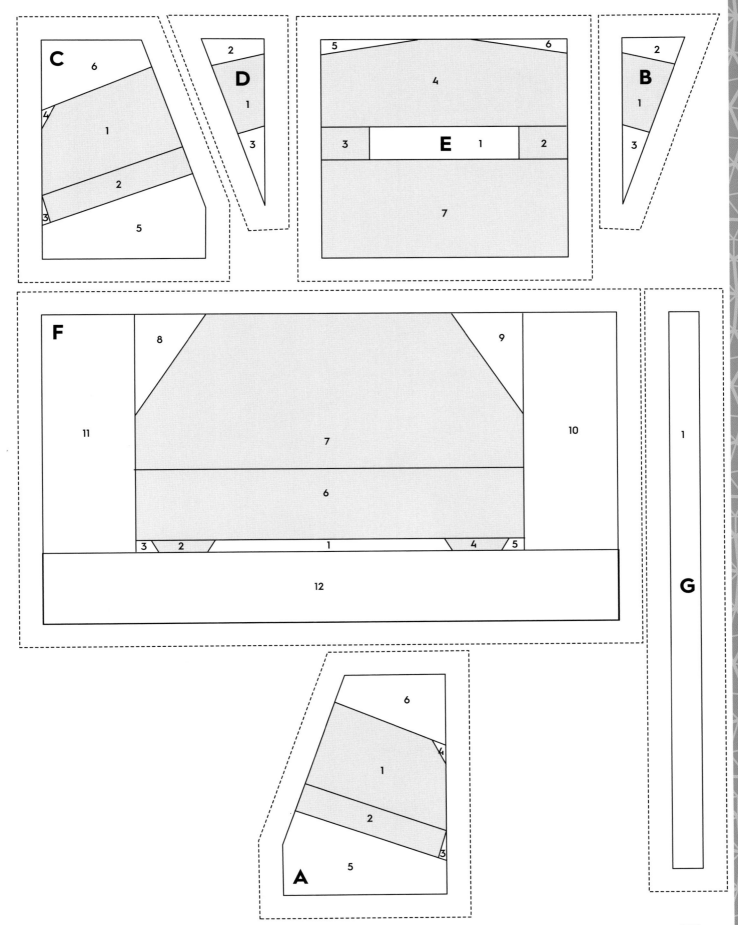

Retro Blooms Coaster

Sarah Ashford

YOU WILL NEED

- One finished Retro Blooms Block (see Garden) made with light grey and assorted pink fabrics
- One piece of coordinating backing fabric, 9" x 9" (23cm x 23cm)
- One piece of wadding, 9" x 9" (23cm x 23cm)
- Single-fold binding fabric strip, 32" x 1½" (81cm x 4cm)

Finished size: approx. 6½" x 6½" (16.5cm x 16.5cm)

All seam allowances are ¼" (6mm) unless stated otherwise.

CONSTRUCTION

1. Place the backing fabric wrong side facing up on your work surface, lay the wadding on top, then place the Retro Blooms Block on top right side facing up. Hold the layers in place using basting spray or tacking stitches as desired. Press well, first on the back, then on the front.

2. Quilt as desired. Here, straight vertical lines have been machine quilted evenly across the panel.

3. Machine stitch all the way around the edge of the coaster to 'seal' the edges prior to binding.

4. Attach the single-fold binding fabric strip to the edge of the coaster following the instructions for Attaching Single-Fold Binding with Mitred Corners (see General Techniques).

Kitten Cushion

Jo Carter

YOU WILL NEED

- One finished Kitten Block (see Creatures)

- Coordinating border fabric: two pieces 4" x 6½" (10cm x 16.5cm) and two pieces 13½" x 4" (34.5cm x 10cm)

- Two pieces of backing fabric, 13½" x 9" (34.5cm x 23cm)

- One piece of lining fabric, 14½" x 14½" (37cm x 37cm)

- One piece of wadding, 14½" x 14½" (37cm x 37cm)

- Cushion pad, 12½" x 12½" (32cm x 32cm)

Finished size: approx. 12½" x 12½" (32cm x 32cm)

All seam allowances are ¼" (6mm) unless otherwise stated.

CONSTRUCTION

1. With right sides facing, pin then sew a 4" x 6½" (10cm x 16.5cm) border strip to the left-hand edge of the Kitten Block. Repeat to attach the second 4" x 6½" (10cm x 16.5cm) border strip to the right-hand side of the block. Press seams towards the border. Join the 13½" x 9" (34.5cm x 23cm) strips to the top and bottom edges to complete the cushion front.

2. Lay the lining fabric wrong side up, centre the wadding on top, then centre the cushion front right side up on top of the wadding. Tack all three layers together using large tacking stitches, safety pins or basting spray.

3. Quilt as desired. Here, a heat-erasable pen was used to draw whiskers on the snout and triangular (stripe) details to the top and sides of the kitten's face. Machine quilt around the eyes, the snout and over the marked lines, then continue around the edge of the kitten.

4. The border was machine quilted in a continuous square spiral with a space of approx. ½" (1.3cm) between the lines.

5. Once the quilting is complete, trim the cushion front to 13½" x 13½" (34.5cm x 34.5cm).

6. Now to make the envelope backing. Start by hemming one of the long edges on each of the two pieces of backing fabric. To do this, fold over the edge by ½" (1.3cm) to the wrong side and press to hold in place. Repeat for a double folded hem, then sew close to the edge of the first fold.

7. Place one of the hemmed backing pieces to the top edge of the cushion front, right sides facing and raw edges aligning, and pin in place. Now pin the remaining hemmed backing piece to the bottom edge of the cushion front. Note that the hemmed edges of the backing pieces overlap in the centre of the cushion. Using a ½" (1.3cm) seam allowance, sew all the way around the cushion to join the back and front together.

8. Clip the seam allowance at the corners and, if desired, zigzag stitch the raw edges to neaten. Turn the cushion cover to the right side and insert the cushion pad.

Lemonade Zipped Purse

Lindsay Chieco

YOU WILL NEED

* Your chosen fabrics to make the Lemonade Block (see Food & Drink for measurements)

* Additional block background fabric: one piece 1" x 6½" (2.5cm x 16.5cm), two pieces 2" x 7" (5cm x 18cm), one piece 7" x 9½" (18cm x 24cm) and two pieces 1" x 3" (2.5cm x 7.5cm)

* Two pieces of linen fabric, 5" x 9½" (13cm x 24cm)

* Two pieces of lining fabric, 11½" x 9½" (29.5cm x 24cm)

* Two pieces of fusible fleece, 11½" x 9½" (29.5cm x 24cm)

* Two pieces of yellow crochet trim, 9½" (24cm) long

* 8" (20.5cm) zip (measuring stopper to stopper)

* One piece of shoestring leather (or narrow ribbon), approx. 3" (8cm) long

Finished size: approx. 9" x 9" (23cm x 23cm)

All seam allowances are ¼" (6mm) unless otherwise stated.

CONSTRUCTION

1. Make up the Lemonade Block using your chosen fabrics.

2. Sew the 1" x 6½" (2.5cm x 16.5cm) piece of additional block background fabric to the top of the block and press seam downwards; then sew the 2" x 7" (5cm x 18cm) pieces to each side of the block and press seams outwards. Your block should now measure 7" x 9½" (18cm x 24cm).

3. To complete the front panel, sew one of the pieces of 5" x 9½" (13cm x 24cm) linen fabric to the bottom of the block, right sides facing, sandwiching the crochet trim in between. Press seam open.

4. To make the back panel, sew the 7" x 9½" (18cm x 24cm) piece of additional block background fabric to the remaining piece of linen fabric, again sandwiching the crochet trim in between. Press seam open.

5. Following the manufacturer's instructions, attach the fusible fleece pieces to the wrong sides of the front and back panels, then quilt as desired. Here, a crisscross pattern has been machine quilted over the back panel, and stitch in the ditch quilting around the lemonade glass on the front panel.

6. Measure and cut a 2" (5cm) square from each corner of the bottom edge of the front and back panels (i.e. from the linen fabric), and from the bottom corners of each piece of the lining fabric also.

7. To make the zip tabs, fold the 1" x 3" (2.5cm x 7.5cm) pieces of additional block background fabric in half (short ends meet, wrong sides facing) and press. Take one piece and sew it along its folded edge to one end of your zip. (Note: the finished length of the zip band needs to be 9½" (24cm).)

8. Place the front panel right side up, then place the zip band right side down (zip closed with pull towards the left) to align with the top edge. Place a piece of lining fabric right side down on top and use a zipper foot to sew through all three layers along the top edge. Fold the front panel and lining fabric away from the zip so now wrong sides are facing, and press.

9. Place the back panel right side up. Place the unsewn edge of the zip right side down, (zip closed with pull towards the right) to align it with the top edge of the back panel. Place the remaining piece of lining fabric right side down on top and use a zipper foot to stitch through all three layers; fold back and press as before.

10. Now line up the front and back (outer) panels, right sides facing, and pin in place. Do the same for the lining panels, but make sure your zip is now half open. Sew across the bottom edge of the outer panels. Sew up each side of the outer panels and each side of the lining panels. Sew across the bottom edge of the lining panels, leaving a 3" (8cm) opening for turning. Note: do not sew along the edge of the cut out corners yet.

11. Working first on the outer panels, bring the side and bottom seams together at each cut out corner. Flatten the fabric to match up the seams, right sides facing, then sew across to close the corner. This creates the box shape at the base of the purse. Repeat to close the corners on the lining panels.

12. Turn the purse right side out through the opening in the lining and press well, then stitch the opening closed. Push the lining inside the purse through the open zip.

13. Feed the shoestring leather through the zip pull and tie a knot to secure it in place.

Sunglasses Tote

Charise Randell

YOU WILL NEED

- One finished Sunglasses Block (see Weather)

- Additional block background fabric: two pieces 1¾" x 6½" (4.5cm x 16.5cm) and two pieces 1¾" x 9" (4.5cm x 23cm)

- Outer fabric: two pieces 18¾" x 17¼" (45.5cm x 44cm) and one piece 8¾" x 8¾" (22.5cm x 22.5cm)

- Two pieces of lining fabric, 18¾" x 17¼" (45.5cm x 44cm)

- Two pieces of sew-in foam stabiliser, 18¾" x 17¼" (45.5cm x 44cm)

- One piece of wadding, 9" x 9" (23cm x 23cm)

- Polka dot bias binding tape, 41" x ½" (105cm x 1.3cm)

- Two ¾" (2cm) wide readymade leather handles, approx. 24"–28" (60cm–70cm) long

Finished size: approx. 17½" (45cm) wide by 14" (35.5cm) tall

All seam allowances are ¼" (6mm) unless otherwise stated.

CONSTRUCTION

NOTE: Back stitch at the beginning and end of each seam.

1. Measure and cut a 2½" (6.5cm) square from the bottom corners of the 18¾" x 17¼" (45.5cm x 44cm) pieces of outer fabric, lining fabric and sew-in foam stabiliser (see Fig. 1).

2. Place each of the outer fabric pieces with cut corners on top of each of the sew-in foam stabiliser pieces so that they are aligned, and tack together ¼" (6mm) from the edge all the way around. These are the front and back panels of the tote.

3. Machine quilt the front and back panels with diagonal lines approx. 2" (5cm) apart.

4. Place the quilted front and back panels together, right sides facing and stitch along the bottom edge with a ⅜" (1cm) seam allowance. Press seam open, then with the joined panels opened out, top stitch along each side of the seam, a ¼" (6mm) away.

5. With right sides facing, stitch the 1¾" x 6½" (4.5cm x 16.5cm) pieces of additional block background fabric to the top and bottom of the Sunglasses Block, and then stitch the 1¾" x 9" (4.5cm x 23cm) pieces to either side. Place the wadding on the wrong side of the enlarged block and tack together ¼" (6mm) from the edge. Machine quilt with stitch in the ditch quilting around the sunglasses. Trim the block to 8¾" (22.5cm) square.

6. Place the 8¾" (22.5cm) square of outer fabric and the enlarged Sunglasses Block together, right sides facing and raw edges aligning, and pin in place. Stitch around the edge with a ⅜" (1cm) seam allowance, leaving a 4" (10cm) opening at the bottom. Turn right side out, fold in the raw edges at the opening and press.

7. Centre the Sunglasses Block on one of the outer panels about 4⅛" (10.5cm) from the bottom seam and top stitch in place, leaving the top edge open to form a pocket.

8. Fold the front/back panel in half, right sides facing, and stitch the sides together with a ⅜" (1cm) seam allowance, from the top edge to the edge of the cut out corners (do not stitch the corners yet). Press seam open, then top stitch ¼" (6mm) away from the seam on either side.

9. Bring the side and bottom seams together at each cut out corner. Flatten the fabric to match up the seams, right sides facing, then sew across with a ⅜" (1cm) seam allowance to close the corner (see Fig. 2). This creates the box shape at the base of the tote. Turn the tote through to the right side.

10. Working with the lining fabric pieces, repeat steps 4, 8 and 9 to make the lining. Place the lining inside the tote so that wrong sides are facing, matching raw edges and seams. Pin in place, then tack all around the top, ¼" (6mm) from the edge.

11. Working on one side of the tote at a time, securely stitch the strap tabs of the readymade leather handles 3½" (9cm) from the top edge and approx. 7¾" (19.5cm) apart.

12. Starting on a side seam, attach the bias binding tape all the way around the top edge of the tote (see General Techniques).

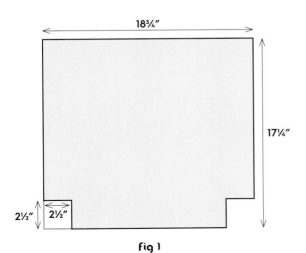

18¾"

17¼"

2½"   2½"

fig 1

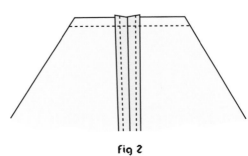

fig 2

Rainy Day Hoop Art

Lindsay Chieco

YOU WILL NEED

- Fabric requirements for the Umbrella Block increased by 50% (see Weather)

- Additional block background fabric: two pieces 1½" x 9½" (4cm x 24.5cm) and two pieces 1½" x 11½" (4cm x 29.5cm)

- One piece of medium-weight fusible interfacing, 11½" x 11½" (29.5cm x 29.5cm)

- 9" (23cm) embroidery hoop

- One piece of fabric (or ribbon), approx. 1½" x 8" (4cm x 20.5cm)

- One piece of felt, 10" x 10" (25.5cm x 25.5cm)

- Blue embroidery thread

Finished size: 9" (23cm) diameter

All seam allowances are ¼" (6mm) unless otherwise stated.

CONSTRUCTION

1. Print off the Umbrella Block patterns at 150% and make up using your chosen fabrics.

2. Sew the 1½" x 9½" (4cm x 24.5cm) pieces of additonal block background fabric to the top and bottom of the finished block and press seams downwards. Sew the 1½" x 11½" (4cm x 29.5cm) pieces to each side of the finished block and press seams outwards. Your work should now measure 11½" x 11½" (29.5cm x 29.5cm).

3. Following the manufacturer's instructions, iron the fusible interfacing onto the back of the block and quilt as desired. Here, the outline of the umbrella was machine quilted first. Then diagonal lines (representing falling rain) were marked 1½" (4cm) apart, using a ruler and a heat-erasable pen and avoiding the umbrella itself. These were embroidered with running stitch worked with two strands of blue embroidery thread (see General Techniques). Once complete, press to remove any remaining pen guide lines.

4. Centre your finished piece between the inner and outer rings of the embroidery hoop and tighten the screw, making sure to pull the fabric taut as you do so. Turn the hoop to the wrong side and cut off the excess fabric about 1" (2.5cm) from the edge. Run a thin line of all-purpose glue around the inside edge of the inner ring of the embroidery hoop, then start to fold over the excess fabric so it sticks to the hoop, working all the way around. Allow the glue to dry.

5. To make a backing, use the embroidery hoop to trace a circle onto the felt and cut it out. Working on the back of the hoop, run a thin line of glue around the glued down excess fabric and press the felt circle on top. Let the glue dry, then cut off any excess felt visible from the front.

6. To make a hanger, take your 1½" x 8" (4cm x 20.5cm) length of fabric (or ribbon), feed it beneath the embroidery hoop screw and tie the ends in a knot.

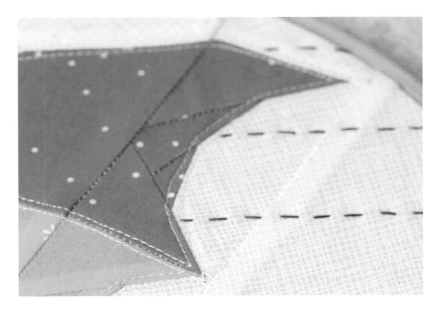

Rainbow Drawstring Pouch

Susan White

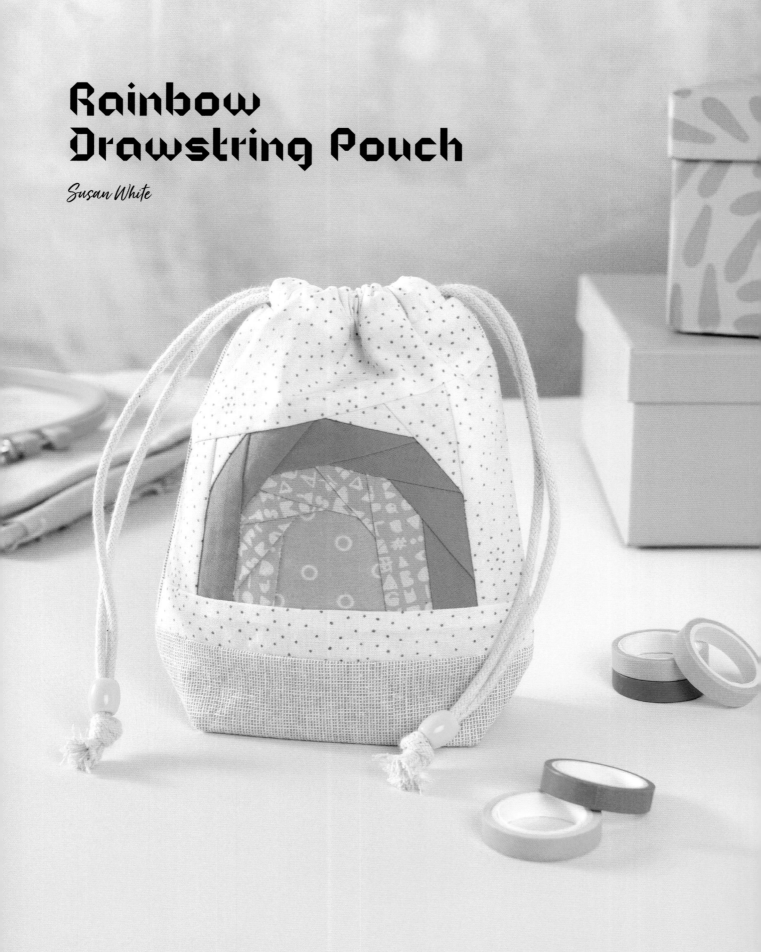

YOU WILL NEED

- Your chosen fabrics to make the Rainbow Block (see Weather for measurements)

- Two pieces of additional block background fabric, 6½" x 2" (16.5cm x 5cm)

- Coordinating fabric: one piece 6½" x 2¾" (16.5cm x 7cm) and one piece 6½" x 7¾" (16.5cm x 19.5cm)

- Two pieces of lining fabric, 6½" x 7¾" (16.5cm x 19.5cm)

- Two pieces of lightweight fusible interfacing, 6½" x 7¾" (16.5cm x 19.5cm)

- Two pieces of cord, approx. 24" (61cm) long

- Two beads (optional)

Finished size: approx 6" (15.5cm) wide by 7" (18cm) tall

All seam allowances are ¼" (6mm) unless otherwise stated.

CONSTRUCTION

1. Make up the Rainbow Block using your chosen fabrics, then measure and cut a 1" (2.5cm) strip from the bottom edge.

2. Sew the 6½" x 2¾" (16.5cm x 7cm) piece of coordinating fabric to the bottom of the block to complete the front panel.

3. Following the manufacturer's instructions, fuse the lightweight fusible interfacing pieces to the wrong side of the pieced front panel and the 6½" x 7¾" (16.5cm x 19.5cm) piece of coordinating fabric, which is the back panel.

4. To prepare the fabric for the drawstring channels, take one of the 6½" x 2" (16.5cm x 5cm) pieces of additional block background fabric and hem the short ends: fold over to the wrong side by ¼" (6mm) and press, then fold over another ¼" (6mm) and press again; top stitch the folded hems in place. Fold the hemmed fabric in half lengthwise, wrong sides facing, and press. Repeat with the remaining piece of additional block background fabric.

5. Place the front panel right side up. Lay one of the prepared drawstring channel pieces so it is centred along the top edge with raw edges aligned. Place one of the 6½" x 7¾" (16.5cm x 19.5cm) pieces of lining fabric right side down on top and pin in place. Sew along the top edge. Open out the assembled pieces and press.

6. Repeat step 5 to join the back panel to the remaining prepared drawstring channel piece and interfaced lining fabric piece.

7. Place the assembled pieces right sides facing, so that the outer fabrics are matched to each other, as are the lining fabrics, and pin in place. Sew around the edge of the matched up panels, leaving a 2" (5cm) opening for turning along the bottom edge of the lining.

8. Working on each of the four corners in turn, pull the fabric apart and pinch the seams together. Pin in place. Measure 1" (2.5cm) from the start of the seam and draw a 2" (5cm) perpendicular line. Sew along the line. Trim the corner, leaving a ¼" (6mm) seam allowance. This forms the rounded shape at the base of the pouch.

9. Turn the pouch right side out through the opening in the lining and press well, then slip stitch the opening closed. Push the lining inside the pouch.

10. Thread the cords through the drawstring channels, add beads if you choose to, then tie the ends in a knot.

Home Sweet Home Table Runner

Sarah Ashford

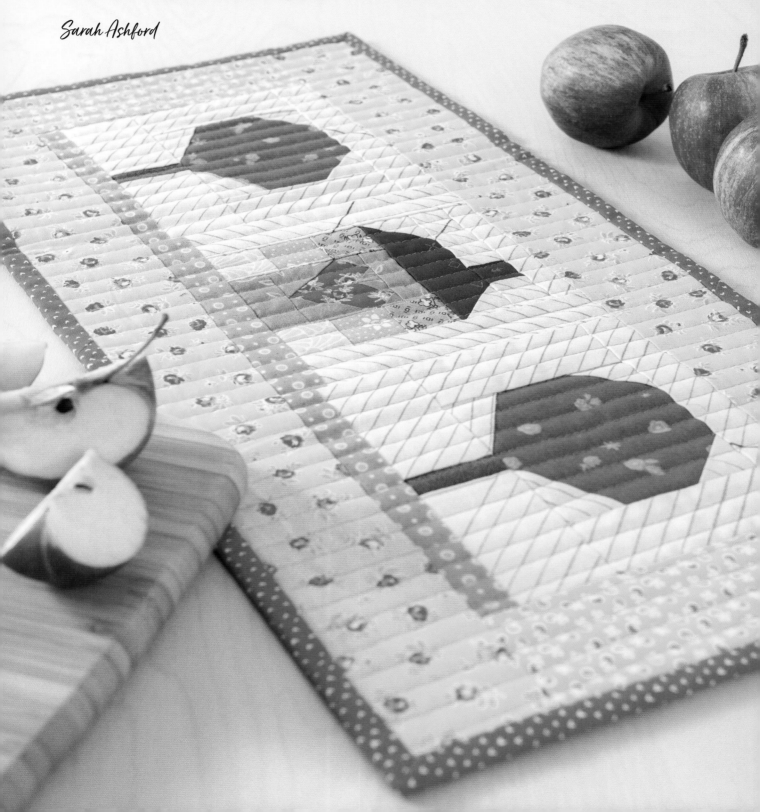

YOU WILL NEED

- Your chosen fabrics to make two of the Tree Block and one New Home Block (see Garden and Celebrations for measurements)

- Coordinating border fabric: two pieces 6½" x 2½" (16.5cm x 6.5cm) and two pieces 22½" x 2½" (57cm x 6.5cm)

- One piece of backing fabric, 24" x 13" (61cm x 33cm)

- One piece of wadding, 24" x 13" (61cm x 33cm)

- Single-fold binding fabric strip, 68" x 1¾" (173cm x 4.5cm)

Finished size: approx. 22½" x 11" (57cm x 28cm)

All seam allowances are ¼" (6mm) unless otherwise stated.

CONSTRUCTION

1. Join a Tree Block to either side of the New Home Block to form the centre panel of the table runner.

2. With right sides facing, pin then sew a 6½" x 2½" (16.5cm x 6.5cm) border strip to the short edges of the centre panel.

3. With right sides facing, pin then sew a 22½" x 2½" (57cm x 6.5cm) border strip to the long edges of the centre panel to complete the top panel.

4. Place the backing fabric wrong side facing up onto your work surface, layer the wadding on top, then place the front panel right side facing up. To hold the layers in place use basting spray or tacking stitches as preferred, and press well, first on the back, then on the front.

5. Quilt as desired. Here, straight vertical lines have been machine quilted evenly across the panel.

6. Once the quilting is complete, trim the edges of the table runner so that they are even, then stitch all the way around the edge to 'seal' the edges.

7. Attach the single-fold binding fabric strip to the edge of the table runner following the instructions for Attaching Single-Fold Binding with Mitred Corners (see General Techniques).

Kitchen Motifs
Apron

Susan White

YOU WILL NEED

* Four finished blocks of your choosing (see Kitchen)

* Floral fabric: one piece 24½" x 4½" (62.5cm x 11.5cm), one piece 24½" x 6½" (62.5cm x 16.5cm) and one piece 24½" x 16½" (62.5cm x 42cm)

* Two pieces of coordinating fabric, 44" x 4½" (112cm x 11.5cm)

* Lightweight fusible interfacing: one piece 24½" x 4½" (62.5cm x 11.5cm), one piece 24½" x 6½" (62.5cm x 16.5cm) and one piece 24½" x 16½" (62.5cm x 42cm)

Finished size: approx. 24" x 16" (61cm x 40.5cm)

All seam allowances are ¼" (6mm) unless otherwise stated.

CONSTRUCTION

1. Following the manufacturer's instructions, fuse the lightweight fusible interfacing pieces to the wrong side of the matching floral fabric pieces.

2. Sew your four finished blocks together to form the centre panel of the apron.

3. To complete the apron's front panel, sew the 24½" x 4½" (62.5cm x 11.5cm) interfaced floral fabric piece to the top edge of the centre panel and the 24½" x 6½" (62.5cm x 16.5cm) interfaced floral fabric piece to the bottom edge.

4. Now make the waist ties. Take one of the 44" x 4½" (112cm x 11.5cm) pieces of coordinating fabric, fold it in half lengthwise with right sides facing, and press. Sew along the edge of the long unfolded side and one short end. Turn right side out and press. Repeat to make the second tie.

5. Lay the 24½" x 16½" (62.5cm x 42cm) piece of floral fabric right side up on your work surface. This is the back panel of your apron.

6. Place one waist tie ½" (1.3cm) down from the top left-hand corner, matching up raw edges. Place the second tie ½" (1.3cm) down from the top right-hand corner, matching up raw edges.

7. Place the front panel right side down on top of the back panel: both waist ties should be inside the fabric sandwich at this point. Pin in place. Sew all the way around the edge, leaving a 4" (10cm) opening along the bottom edge for turning through.

8. Turn the apron right side out through the opening and press. Fold in the raw edges at the opening, then top stitch all the way around the edge of the apron.

The waist ties are designed to be wrapped to the front in a cute bow, but if you prefer to tie them at the back, you might want to consider making them shorter.

Cottage Craft Basket

Charise Randell

CONSTRUCTION

NOTE: Back stitch at the beginning and end of each seam.

1. Following the manufacturer's instructions, fuse four of the 8¾" (22.5cm) fusible wadding squares to the wrong side of each of the 8¾" (22.5cm) linen fabric squares, .

2. Stitch the 1¾" x 6½" (4.5cm x 16.5cm) pieces of additional linen fabric to the top and bottom of the Cottage Block, with right sides facing; then stitch the 1¾" x 9" (4.5cm x 23cm) pieces to the sides. Fuse the remaining 8¾" (22.5cm) square of fusible wadding to the wrong side of the enlarged block.

3. Place a canvas square over the fusible wadding on the wrong side of the enlarged Cottage Block and tack together ¼" (6mm) from the edge. Machine quilt with stitch in the ditch quilting on the cottage seams and echo quilting around the outside of the cottage, using matching thread. This is the front panel of the craft basket.

4. Place a canvas square over the fusible wadding on each of the four additional linen fabric squares and tack together ¼" (6mm) from the edge. Machine quilt each panel with diagonal lines of stitching approx. 1¾" (4.5cm) apart. These are the side, back and base panels of the craft basket.

5. Place a side panel on to the front panel, right sides facing, and stitch together along one side using a ⅜" (1cm) seam allowance, starting at the top edge and ending ⅜" (1cm) from the bottom. Repeat to sew a side panel to the other side of the front panel.

6. Referring to step 5, stitch the back panel to either side panel. You should now have something that resembles a box.

7. Pin the base panel to the front panel along the bottom edge matching raw edges. Stitch the seam starting ⅜" (1cm) from one side seam and ending ⅜" (1cm) from the opposite side seam. Repeat to sew the base to the remaining three sides. Turn right side out and press seams flat.

8. Repeat steps 5–7 to make a lining from the five 8¾" (22.5cm) lining fabric squares. Place the lining inside the craft basket wrong sides facing, matching raw edges and seams. Pin in place, then tack all around the top ¼" (6mm) from the edge.

9. Now to make the ruffle. Start by stitching together the short ends of the polka dot fabric strip to form a circle and press the seam open. Fold the long edges together, wrong sides facing, and press. Sew a long tacking stitch ¼" (6mm) away from the raw edge and pull up to gather.

10. Match the raw edges of the ruffle with the top edge of the basket and redistribute the gathers so they are even. Tack the ruffle in place ¼" (6mm) from the edge (see Fig. 1).

11. Starting at the centre back of the basket, attach the bias binding tape all the way around the top edge of the basket (see General Techniques).

fig 1

Grapefruit Hot Pad

Charise Randell

YOU WILL NEED

- Your chosen fabrics to make the Grapefruit Block (see Fruit for measurements; natural linen was used for the block background fabric)

- Additional linen fabric: two pieces 1¼" x 6½" (3cm x 16.5cm) and two pieces 1¼" x 8" (3cm x 20.5cm)

- One piece of muslin backing fabric, 8½" x 8½" (21.5cm x 21.5cm)

- One piece of fruit print backing fabric, 8½" x 8½" (21.5cm x 21.5cm)

- One piece of coordinating polka dot fabric, 2¾" x 12" (7cm x 30.5cm)

- One piece of heat-resistant wadding, 8½" x 8½" (21.5cm x 21.5cm)

- One piece of cotton wadding, 8½" x 8½" (21.5cm x 21.5cm)

- Gingham bias binding tape, 45" x ½" (115cm x 1.3cm)

Finished size: approx. 8" x 8" (20.5cm x 20.5cm)

All seam allowances are ¼" (6mm) unless otherwise stated.

CONSTRUCTION

1. With right sides facing, stitch the 1¼" x 6½" (3cm x 16.5cm) pieces of additional linen fabric to the top and bottom of the Grapefruit Block, then stitch the 1¼" x 8" (3cm x 20.5cm) pieces to each side.

2. Lay the muslin backing fabric wrong side up, centre the cotton wadding on top, then place the enlarged block right side up on top of the wadding. Tack together ¼" (6mm) from the edge.

3. Machine quilt with stitch in the ditch quilting on the seams of the Grapefruit Block.

4. Place the fruit print backing fabric wrong side up on your work surface, lay the piece of heat-resistant wadding on top, then the front (block) panel right side up on top of the wadding. Tack through all layers working ¼" (6mm) from the raw edge, then trim to 8" x 8" (20.5cm x 20.5cm).

5. To create rounded corners, use a fabric marker pen to trace around the curve of a drinking glass at each corner and cut along the marked lines.

6. To make the hanging loop, cut a 4¾" (12cm) strip of the bias binding tape, edge stitch the folded edges together, then fold in half to make a loop. Place the hanging loop on the back of the hot pad, centring it at the top edge and matching raw edges. Tack in place (see Fig. 1).

7. Now to make the ruffle. Fold the 2¾" x 12" (7cm x 30.5cm) piece of polka dot fabric in half lengthwise, with wrong sides facing. Stitch two lines of tacking stitch ¼" (6mm) and ⅜" (1cm) away from the raw edges. Pull up the lines of stitching to gather.

8. With the block side facing up, align the ruffle to the top edge of the hot pad, so the raw edges match. Redistribute the gathers so they are even, then tack in place. Trim the top edge of the ruffle to match the curve of the corners.

9. Starting at the centre bottom edge of the back panel, attach the bias binding tape all the way around the edge of the hot pad (see General Techniques).

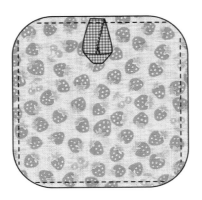

fig 1

GENERAL TECHNIQUES

STITCHES

Running stitch

Starting at the right-hand side, bring the needle out at A and insert it at B. Bring it out again at C and insert it at D. Continue in this way making sure the stitches and gaps are of even length. Tacking stitches, used to temporarily hold fabric layers together, are simply long running stitches approx. ⁵⁄₈" (1.5cm) long.

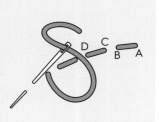

Slip stitch

Work from right to left picking up a tiny piece of the fabric from one seam edge or fabric piece. Insert the needle into the other seam fold or fabric piece and move it along by ⅛" (3mm). Push the needle out and repeat.

Satin stitch

Work straight stitches close together in parallel lines, keeping the tension even throughout to give a smooth, satin look. The aim is to fill in the shape so that none of the background fabric can be seen.

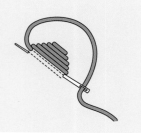

Couching stitch

Work small straight stitches to secure in place a length of thread, for example, laid across the surface of the fabric in a design.

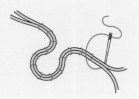

ATTACHING SINGLE-FOLD BINDING WITH MITRED CORNERS

This technique is used to attach the binding to the Home Sweet Home Table Runner and Retro Blooms Coaster. Press a ¼" (6mm) hem along one long edge of your fabric strip. Starting part way along one side of the front of the project, place fabric strip to edge of project, right sides facing and raw edges aligning. Machine stitch to within ¼" (6mm) of edge. Fold fabric strip upwards to make a diagonal fold and fingerpress to hold in place (Fig 1), then fold the fabric strip back down to align with the next edge. Ensuring that the diagonal fold is held in place, continue stitching from the top edge (Fig 2). Repeat at each corner. On reaching the start point, fold over ⅜" (1cm) and slip folded end under raw edge. Now fold the binding to the back of the project and slip stitch in place along the folded edge, folding a neat mitre at each corner.

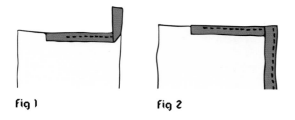

fig 1   fig 2

ATTACHING BIAS BINDING TAPE

This technique is used to attach the binding to the Sunglasses Tote, Cottage Craft Basket and Grapefruit Hot Pad. Fold one end of the bias binding under to the wrong side for ⅜" (1cm) and place this folded end as advised in the project instructions, with right side of the binding to the right side of lining or backing fabric. If using ½" (1.3cm) bias binding tape, stitch ⅜" (1cm) from the edge, and for ⅜" (1cm) bias binding tape, stitch ¼" (6mm) from the edge; on reaching the start point, overlap the folded edge by ½" (1.3cm) and continue stitching. Now fold the bias binding to the right side of the project to just cover the previous stitching line and machine edge stitch or slip stitch by hand, depending on your preference.

MAKING A CIRCLE APPLIQUÉ

Once the paper piecing has been completed, three of the blocks are finished using this technique: fabric circles are appliquéd on to the Kitchen Scales and the Retro Phone to represent the dials and to the Camera for the lens.

Use the appropriate circle pattern(s) to cut one circle from freezer paper on the solid line and one from fabric on the dashed line. Iron the freezer paper circle to the centre of the wrong side of the fabric circle.

Hand stitch a long running stitch around the edge of the fabric circle approx. ⅛" (3mm) away from the raw edge. With wrong side facing up, gather the stitches by gently pulling on the thread ends. Use a cotton bud to apply fabric starch to the gathered edge of the fabric, then carefully iron it over the edge of the freezer paper circle. Loosen the stitches and remove the freezer paper circle. Turn the fabric circle to the right side and press.

Using the block reference diagram as a guide, sew the prepared circle in place, either by machine stitching close to the edge or by hand stitching using an invisible slip stitch.

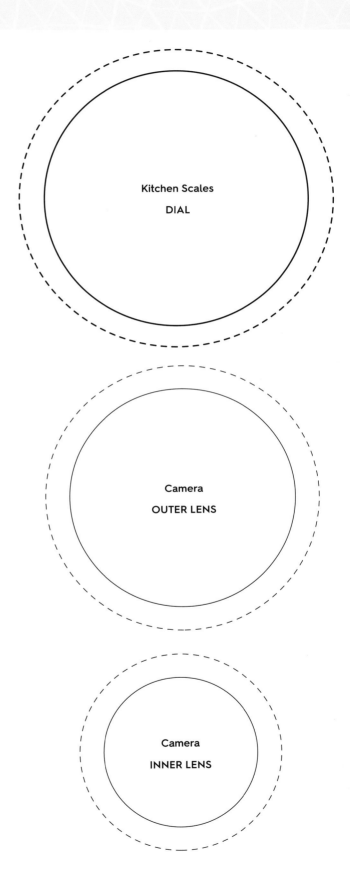

Kitchen Scales
DIAL

Camera
OUTER LENS

Camera
INNER LENS

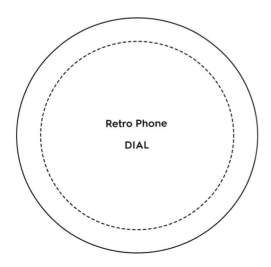

Retro Phone
DIAL

Full-size printable versions of these patterns can be downloaded from www.davidandcharles.com.

THE DESIGNERS

The publisher would like to thank all of the designers whose patterns and projects appear in this book.

Sarah Ashford

Instagram: @sarahashfordstudio

Website: sarahashfordstudio.com

A modern quilter and designer, Sarah is the host of the annual Great British Quilter Instagram Challenge and Podcast, which is now in its second series.

Jo Carter

Instagram: @jo2owls

Website: www.twoowlsdesign.co.uk

Primarily a soft toy designer, Jo's quilt patterns have appeared in several magazines including *Love Patchwork and Quilting*.

Lindsay Chicco

Instagram: @linzentart

A self-taught sewer, Lindsay loves sharing her makes on Instagram, occasionally selling her patterns at www.etsy.com/shop/linzentart.

Kerry Green

Instagram: @verykerryberry

Website: verykerryberry.blogspot.com

A quilter and dressmaker with a vintage aesthetic, who loves bright happy colours, strong graphic shapes and mixing feedsack fabrics with modern prints, Kerry also works as a social media manager for crafty companies.

Joanne Hart

Instagram: @unicornharts

Website: www.unicornharts.com

Addicted to paper piecing, Jo designs patterns to share with fellow sewaholics, available at www.payhip.com/unicornharts.

Monika Henry

Instagram: @pennyspoolquilts

Website: www.pennyspoolquilts.com

A modern quilt pattern designer, Monika loves simple, bright and fun designs, and she hopes to inspire quilting confidence through her patterns and tutorials.

Kristy Lea

Instagram: @quietplay

Website: www.quietplaydesigns.com

A paper pieced pattern and quilting fabric designer, Kristy's designs celebrate a love of rainbow, geometric design and colour.

Charise Randell

Instagram: @charisecreates

Website: www.charisecreates.blogspot.com

An author and designer, Charise has designed women's apparel for over 15 years and spends her days designing sewing and quilting patterns.

Juliet van der Heijden

Instagram: @tartankiwi

Website: www.thetartankiwi.com

A self-taught quilter, Juliet loves the thrill of translating an idea or a picture into a paper pieced design, and many more of designs can be found in her book, *Animal Quilts*.

Susan White

Instagram: @quiltypie

A lover of all things craft, more of Susan's paper pieced patterns can be found at www.etsy.com/shop/quiltypie.

Kitty Wilkin

Instagram: @nightquilter

Website: www.nightquilter.com

With three small kids, Kitty finds her only sewing time is after bedtime, hence her blog, the night quilter, all about her stitching projects and creating her own patterns.

INDEX

A DAVID AND CHARLES BOOK
© David and Charles, Ltd 2021

David and Charles is an imprint of David and Charles, Ltd
Suite A, Tourism House, Pynes Hill, Exeter, EX2 5WS

Text and Designs © David and Charles, Ltd 2021
Layout and Photography © David and Charles, Ltd 2021

First published in the UK and USA in 2021

A catalogue record for this book is available from the British Library.

ISBN-13: 9781446308691 paperback
ISBN-13: 9781446380741 EPUB
ISBN-13: 9781446380734 PDF

This book has been printed on paper from approved suppliers and made from pulp from sustainable sources.

Printed in the UK by Page Bros for:
David and Charles, Ltd
Suite A, Tourism House, Pynes Hill, Exeter, EX2 5WS

10 9 8 7 6 5 4 3 2

Publishing Director: Ame Verso
Senior Commissioning Editor: Sarah Callard
Managing Editor: Jeni Chown
Project Editor: Cheryl Brown
Head of Design: Sam Staddon
Pre-press Designer: Ali Stark
Design and Art Direction: Prudence Rogers
Photography: Jason Jenkins
Production Manager: Beverley Richardson

David and Charles publishes high-quality books on a wide range of subjects.
For more information visit www.davidandcharles.com.

Share your makes with us on social media using #dandcbooks and follow us on Facebook and Instagram by searching for @dandcbooks.

Layout of the digital edition of this book may vary depending on reader hardware and display settings.